ALSO BY OSHO

Tarot in the Spirit of Zen — The Game of Life
The Book of Secrets — 112 Keys to Unlock the Mystery Within
Meditation — The First and Last Freedom
Love Freedom Aloneness — The Koan of Relationships
Sex Matters
Autobiography of a Spiritually Incorrect Mystic
Osho Transformation Tarot
India My Love — A Spiritual Journey
Yoga — The Science of the Soul
Tao — The Pathless Path
Zen — The Path of Paradox
The Art of Tea — Meditations To Awaken Your Spirit

Insights for a New Way of Living series:
Courage — The Joy of Living Dangerously
Creativity — Unleashing the Forces Within
Maturity — The Responsibility of Being Oneself
Awareness — The Key to Living in Balance
Intuition — Knowing beyond Logic
Intimacy — Trusting Oneself and the Other

Zen knows only a vast life
which contains all kinds of contradictions
in a deep harmony.
The night is in harmony with the day,
and life is in harmony with death,
and the earth is in harmony with the sky.
The presence is in harmony with the absence.
This immense harmony,
this synchronicity,
is the essential Manifesto of Zen.
This is the only way of life which respects
and loves,
and denies nothing, condemns nothing.

OSHO: *THE ZEN MANIFESTO*

OSHO®

ZEN

TAROT

THE TRANSCENDENTAL GAME OF ZEN

St. Martin's Press

Original Illustrations by Deva Padma
Edited by Sarito Carol Neiman
Commentaries based on descriptions by Deva Padma
Design by Amiyo Ruhnke & Deva Sandipa
Typesetting and computer graphics by Sambodhi Prem
Production by Kamal

ISBN 0-312-11733-7
First published in Great Britain by Boxtree Limited
Second Edition

10 9

CONTENTS

THE TRANSCENDENTAL GAME OF ZEN

Major Arcana

MINOR ARCANA

MINOR ARCANA

MINOR ARCANA

ACKNOWLEDGEMENTS

Grateful acknowledgement is given to the
following people for helping to create this book:
Anand Zeno
Dhyan Sammadhi
Deva Prem
Deva Ayama
And to Emma Kunz,
for inspiration for the card 'Healing'.
Acknowledgement for glossary
references is given to J.C. Cooper,
*The Illustrated Encyclopaedia of
Traditional Symbols.* Thames & Hudson.

During the course of thirty years of talks to disciples and friends, Osho would answer their questions, or comment on the teachings of the world's great sages and scriptures. His talks continue to bring fresh insight to everything, from obscure Vedic scriptures to the familiar sayings of Jesus. He speaks with equal authority on the Hassids and the Sufis, the Bauls, Yoga and the Buddhists. Ultimately Osho concentrates on transmitting the unique wisdom of Zen, because, he says, Zen is the one spiritual tradition whose approach to the inner life of human beings has weathered the test of time and is still relevant to contemporary humanity.

Unlike other religions, which have fallen prey to hero worship and dogmatism, Zen insists on the unique capacity of every human being to reach enlightenment – or freedom from the illusions of ego created by the mind. And it insists that this capacity can be realized only through meditation. Not by following certain rituals, adhering to a set of rules, or imitating the example of others, however worthy, but only by an alert and non-judgmental attentiveness to one's own thoughts, actions and feelings. When we practice this alertness, this meditative approach to life, it soon brings the awareness that we each contain an unchanging, undisturbed, and eternal center of watchfulness – a center that has the capacity to see life as a great adventure, a play, a mystery school, and, finally, a blissful journey with no purpose other than to delight in every step along the way.

In Osho's words, it is the capacity not to worship buddhas but to *become* a buddha; not to follow others but to develop the awareness within that brings a quality of light and love to all that we do.

Osho has always been more than just an orator or philosopher, however. In the commune of friends that has surrounded him he has created an atmosphere where the truths he speaks of can be directly experienced. To travel the path in the company of Osho is not to retreat to the mountains to lead a life of asceticism and repose, far away from the marketplace. On the contrary, it is to engage oneself totally in the task of waking up, through a rich variety of meditations, physical healing and psychological therapies, lots of laughter and playfulness, and healthy doses of creativity and hard work. Cleaning the floor is as much a meditation as sitting silently in the presence of the master, and confronting the power struggles of one's fellow workers in the kitchen is as significant as understanding the Diamond Sutra spoken by Gautam Buddha. Even the ups and downs of love affairs have their place in the journey to discover who we are.

It is in the context of this approach to life, this commitment to making the whole of life a meditation, that this tarot deck was created. And it is dedicated to the buddha within each and every one of us.

The buddha is nobody's monopoly, it is nobody's copyright. It is everybody's innermost being. You don't have to be a Buddhist to be a buddha. To be a buddha transcends all concepts of religions; it is everybody's birthright. Persuade it to come along with you, to your daily activities, so everything in your life becomes a meditation, a grace, a beauty, a benediction.

OSHO: *NO MIND: THE FLOWERS OF ETERNITY*

Sarito

Tarot has been in existence for thousands of years, since ancient Egypt or perhaps even before. The first known use of the tarot in the West was in the Middle Ages. During those turbulent times, the imagery of the tarot was used as a code in transmitting the teachings of the medieval mystery schools. Over time, tarot has been used in many ways — as a tool for predicting the future, as a lighthearted 'parlor game', a way to gather unseen, 'occult' information about various situations, etcetera.

Some say that the number of cards is based on the number of steps taken by the infant Siddhartha — later to become Gautama the Buddha — as soon as he was born. He walked seven steps forward and seven steps backward in each of the four cardinal directions, says the legend, and this became the model for the 'minor' cards in the tarot.

In addition to these 56 cards of the Minor Arcana, the tarot contains an additional 22 cards, the Major Arcana, which tell the complete story of the human spiritual journey. From the first innocent step of The Fool, to the culmination of the journey represented by the card of Completion, we find in the Major Arcana the archetypal images that connect us all as human beings. They tell of a journey of self-discovery that is absolutely unique to each individual, while the core truths to be discovered are the same regardless of race, gender, class or religious upbringing.

In the traditional tarot deck this journey of self-discovery was perceived as a kind of spiral, with each Completion leading to a new level on the path, a new beginning with the re-entry of The Fool. In this deck, however, the Master card has been added. This card allows us to leave the spiral behind, to take a jump off the wheel of death and rebirth. The Master card symbolizes the ultimate transcendence of journeying itself, a transcendence that becomes possible only through the dissolving of the separate, individual ego in enlightenment.

Osho Zen Tarot is definitely not a traditional tarot in the sense that you play with prediction. Rather it is a transcendental game of Zen which mirrors the moment, unwaveringly presenting what is here, now, without judgment or comparison. This game is a wake-up call to tune in to sensitivity, intuition, compassion, receptivity, courage and individuality.

This focus on awareness is one of the many innovations to the old systems and thinking of the tarot that will soon become obvious to experienced users as they begin to work with the Osho Zen Tarot.

THE MAJOR ARCANA

These 22 cards are numbered with roman numerals from 0 to XXI in this deck and represent the central, archetypal themes of the human spiritual journey. The Master card, symbolizing transcendence, has no number.

When a Major Arcana card appears in a reading, it has special significance above and beyond the cards of the Minor Arcana. It tells us that our current circumstances are giving us an opportunity to examine one of the central themes of our own individual spiritual journey. It will be particularly helpful to examine other cards in reference to this central theme — for example, "What does the fact that I've been working too hard (Exhaustion) tell me about my need for self-expression (Creativity)? How am I thwarting my progress in the journey towards creativity by putting all my energy into keeping the 'machine' going?

If there are no Major Arcana cards in the reading, chances are the current situation is a transient sub-plot of the larger play of your life. This doesn't mean that it is unimportant, or that you should feel foolish to be so strongly affected by it, but the very absence of Major Arcana cards can reassure you that 'this too will pass', and later on you might very well wonder what all the fuss was about.

Finally, if there are Major Arcana cards in a reading it can indicate that a major change of scenes and characters in the play is taking place. There are times, in fact, when the profusion of Major Arcana cards is so overwhelming that you might want to choose just one of them – the one that strikes you with the clearest message – as the centerpiece of a new reading to help you understand what you are facing now.

THE MINOR ARCANA

These 56 cards are divided into four suits representing the four elements, each marked with a particular color-coded diamond to distinguish them, and of the predominant color of the suit. The cards of the Water suit have a blue diamond, those of Fire, red, Clouds have a gray diamond, and Rainbows, a rainbow-colored diamond. As in a regular deck of playing cards, the suits of the tarot each contain 'court cards' which have here been stripped of the importance of their aristocratic feudal titles and given names to simply represent the different oportunities for mastery over the four elements that they occupy.

The suit of Fire corresponds to the Wands of the traditional tarot, and represents the realm of action and response, the energy that moves us into situations and out of them again when we follow our 'gut feelings' rather than our minds or our emotions.

The Water suit replaces the traditional Cups, representing the emotional side of life, and tends to be a more 'feminine' and receptive energy than Fire, which is more 'masculine' and outgoing.

Clouds have been chosen to replace Swords, traditionally the suit of air, representing the mind. This is because the nature of the unenlightened mind is precisely cloud-like in the way it blocks light and darkens the landscape around us, preventing us from seeing things as they really are. But there is another aspect to clouds that must not be overlooked – they come and go, and are therefore not to be taken too seriously!

Finally, the suit of Rainbows in this deck takes the place of the traditional suit of Disks, or Pentacles, representing the earth element. This is traditionally the element representing the practical, material side of life. But in keeping with the attitude of Zen, that even the most humble, earthy activities contain an opportunity to celebrate the sacred, the Rainbow has been chosen for this suit. In using the Rainbow – which bridges the earth and sky, matter and spirit – we remind ourselves that in reality there is no separation between the lower and the higher, that indeed it is a continuum of one total energy. And that heaven is not some remote place high in the sky, but a reality waiting to be discovered right here on earth.

So here is a journey of discovery, and the way to the ultimate transcendence of it all. Go lightly and playfully, from the peaks to the valleys and back to the peaks again, savoring every step of the way. Learn from your mistakes and you can't go wrong.

Obviously you can ask the tarot what you like, although it is in fact a vehicle for exposing what you already know. Any card drawn in response to an issue is a direct reflection of what you are sometimes unable or unwilling to recognize at this time. And yet it is only through recognition (without judging as right or wrong) from a detached perspective that you can begin to fully experience your height and depth – all the colors of our rainbow being.

When consulting the 'mirror' of the tarot, shuffle the cards well, imagining them as a receptacle into which you are pouring your energies. When you feel ready, fan them face down, and using your left hand (the receptive), select cards in response to your present issue. Remember to stay in the moment as you turn the cards over, allowing your inner responses to clarify your outer issues.

As you will experience, the images of the Osho Zen Tarot are alive. Their impact is undeniable, for they speak to us in a language that our deeper selves recognize. They awaken understanding. They provoke clarity.

Included in the back of the book are a few spreads or layouts to play with (see page 160), but ultimately you will develop your own way of using the cards. Be creative – the possibilities are limitless.

Be as silent and focused as possible when you are using this deck. The more you are able to perceive the process as a gift for your individual growth, the more meaningful the messages will be for you.

M oment to moment, and with every step, the Fool leaves the past behind. He carries nothing more than his purity, innocence and trust, symbolized by the white rose in his hand. The pattern on his waistcoat contains the colors of all four elements of the tarot, indicating that he is in harmony with all that surrounds him. His intuition is functioning at its peak. At this moment the Fool has the support of the universe to make this jump into the unknown. Adventures await him in the river of life. ✦ The card indicates that if you trust your intuition right now, your feeling of the 'rightness' of things, you cannot go wrong. Your actions may appear 'foolish' to others, or even to yourself, if you try to analyze them with the rational mind. But the 'zero' place occupied by the Fool is the numberless number where trust and innocence are the guides, not skepticism and past experience.

THE FOOL

✦   ✦   ✦

A FOOL IS ONE who goes on trusting; a fool is one who goes on trusting against all his experience. You deceive him, and he trusts you; and you deceive him again, and he trusts you; and you deceive him again, and he trusts you. Then you will say that he is a fool, he does not learn. His trust is tremendous; his trust is so pure that nobody can corrupt it.

Be a fool in the Taoist sense, in the Zen sense. Don't try to create a wall of knowledge around you. Whatsoever experience comes to you, let it happen, and then go on dropping it. Go on cleaning your mind continuously; go on dying to the past so you remain in the present, here-now, as if just born, just a babe. In the beginning it is going to be very difficult. The world will start taking advantage of you…let them. They are poor fellows. Even if you are cheated and deceived and robbed, let it happen, because that which is really yours cannot be robbed from you, that which is really yours nobody can steal from you. And each time you don't allow situations to corrupt you, that opportunity will become an integration inside. Your soul will become more crystallized.[1]

T his naked figure sits on the lotus leaf of perfection, gazing at the beauty of the night sky. She knows that 'home' is not a physical place in the outside world, but an inner quality of relaxation and acceptance. The stars, the rocks, the trees, the flowers, fish and birds – all are our brothers and sisters in this dance of life. We human beings tend to forget this, as we pursue our own private agendas and believe we must fight to get what we need. But ultimately, our sense of separateness is just an illusion, manufactured by the narrow preoccupations of the mind. ✦ Now is the time to look at whether you are allowing yourself to receive the extraordinary gift of feeling 'at home' wherever you are. If you are, be sure to take time to savor it so it can deepen and remain with you. If on the other hand you've been feeling like the world is out to get you, it's time to take a break. Go outside tonight and look at the stars.

EXISTENCE

✦   ✦   ✦

YOU ARE NOT accidental. Existence needs you. Without you something will be missing in existence and nobody can replace it. That's what gives you dignity, that the whole existence will miss you. The stars and sun and moon, the trees and birds and earth – everything in the universe will feel a small place is vacant which cannot be filled by anybody except you. This gives you a tremendous joy, a fulfillment that you are related to existence, and existence cares for you. Once you are clean and clear, you can see tremendous love falling on you from all dimensions.[2]

The Inner Voice speaks not in words but in the wordless language of the heart. It is like an oracle who only speaks the truth. If it had a face, it would be like the face at the center of this card – alert, watchful, and able to accept both the dark and the light, symbolized by the two hands holding the crystal. The crystal itself represents the clarity that comes from transcending all dualities. The Inner Voice can also be playful, as it dives deep into the emotions and emerges again to soar towards the sky, like two dolphins dancing in the waters of life. It is connected with the cosmos, through the crescent-moon crown, and the earth, as represented by the green leaves on the figure's kimono. ✦ There are times in our lives when too many voices seem to be pulling us this way and that. Our very confusion in such situations is a reminder to seek silence and centering within. Only then are we able to hear our truth.

INNER VOICE

✦　　✦　　✦

IF YOU HAVE FOUND your truth within yourself there is nothing more in this whole existence to find. Truth is functioning through you. When you open your eyes, it is truth opening his eyes. When you close your eyes, it is truth who is closing its eyes.

This is a tremendous meditation. If you can simply understand the device, you don't have to do anything; whatever you are doing is being done by truth. You are walking, it is truth; you are sleeping, it is truth resting; you are speaking, it is truth speaking; you are silent, it is truth that is silent.

This is one of the most simple meditation techniques. Slowly, slowly everything settles by this simple formula, and then there is no need for the technique.

When you are cured, you throw away the meditation, you throw away the medicine. Then you live as truth – alive, radiant, contented, blissful, a song unto yourself. Your whole life becomes a prayer without any words, or better to say a prayerfulness, a grace, a beauty which does not belong to our mundane world, a ray of light coming from the beyond into the darkness of our world. [3]

From the alchemy of fire and water below to the divine light entering from above, the figure in this card is literally 'possessed by' the creative force. Really, the experience of creativity is an entry into the mysterious. Technique, expertise and knowledge are just tools; the key is to abandon oneself to the energy that fuels the birth of all things. This energy has no form or structure, yet all the forms and structures come out of it.

◆ It makes no difference what particular form your creativity takes — it can be painting or singing, planting a garden or making a meal. The important thing is to be open to what wants to be expressed through you. Remember that we don't possess our creations; they do not belong to us. True creativity arises from a union with the divine, with the mystical and the unknowable. Then it is both a joy for the creator and a blessing to others.

CREATIVITY

✦   ✦   ✦

REATIVITY IS THE QUALITY that you bring to the activity that you are doing. It is an attitude, an inner approach – how you look at things.... Not everybody can be a painter – and there is no need also. If everybody is a painter the world will be very ugly; it will be difficult to live. And not everybody can be a dancer, and there is no need. But everybody can be creative.

Whatsoever you do, if you do it joyfully, if you do it lovingly, if your act of doing is not purely economical, then it is creative. If you have something growing out of it within you, if it gives you growth, it is spiritual, it is creative, it is divine.

You become more divine as you become more creative. All the religions of the world have said God is the creator. I don't know whether he is the creator or not, but one thing I know: the more creative you become, the more godly you become. When your creativity comes to a climax, when your whole life becomes creative, you live in God. So he must be the creator because people who have been creative have been closest to him.

Love what you do. Be meditative while you are doing it – whatsoever it is![4]

COMMENTARY

The powerful and authoritative figure in this card is clearly the master of his own destiny. On his shoulder is an emblem of the sun, and the torch he holds in his right hand symbolizes the light of his own hard-won truth. Whether he is wealthy or poor, the Rebel is really an emperor because he has broken the chains of society's repressive conditioning and opinions. He has formed himself by embracing all the colors of the rainbow, emerging from the dark and formless roots of his unconscious past and growing wings to fly into the sky. His very way of being is rebellious — not because he is fighting against anybody or anything, but because he has discovered his own true nature and is determined to live in accordance with it. The eagle is his spirit animal, a messenger between earth and sky. ✦ The Rebel challenges us to be courageous enough to take responsibility for who we are and to live our truth.

THE REBEL

✦ ✦ ✦

PEOPLE ARE AFRAID, very much afraid of those who know themselves. They have a certain power, a certain aura and a certain magnetism, a charisma that can take out alive, young people from the traditional imprisonment....

The enlightened man cannot be enslaved – that is the difficulty – and he cannot be imprisoned....

Every genius who has known something of the inner is bound to be a little difficult to be absorbed; he is going to be an upsetting force. The masses don't want to be disturbed, even though they may be in misery; they are in misery, but they are accustomed to the misery. And anybody who is not miserable looks like a stranger.

The enlightened man is the greatest stranger in the world; he does not seem to belong to anybody. No organization confines him, no community, no society, no nation.[5]

Being 'in the gap' can be disorienting and even scary. Nothing to hold on to, no sense of direction, not even a hint of what choices and possibilities might lie ahead. But it was just this state of pure potential that existed before the universe was created. All you can do now is to relax into this no-thingness...fall into this silence between the words...watch this gap between the outgoing and incoming breath. And treasure each empty moment of the experience. Something sacred is about to be born.

NO-THINGNESS

✦ ✦ ✦

BUDDHA HAS CHOSEN one of the really very potential words – *shunyata*. The English word, the English equivalent, 'nothingness', is not such a beautiful word.

That's why I would like to make it 'no-thingness' – because the nothing is not just nothing, it is all. It is vibrant with all possibilities. It is potential, absolute potential. It is unmanifest yet, but it contains all.

In the beginning is nature, in the end is nature, so why in the middle do you make so much fuss? Why, in the middle, becoming so worried, so anxious, so ambitious – why create such despair?

Nothingness to nothingness is the whole journey.[6]

W hat we call love is really a whole spectrum of relating, reaching from the earth to the sky. At the most earthy level, love is sexual attraction. Many of us remain stuck there, because our conditioning has burdened our sexuality with all kinds of expectations and repressions. Actually the biggest 'problem' with sexual love is that it never lasts. Only if we accept this fact can we then really celebrate it for what it is — welcome its happening, and say good-bye with gratitude when it's not. Then as we mature, we can begin to experience the love that exists beyond sexuality and honors the unique individuality of the other. We begin to understand that our partner often functions as a mirror, reflecting unseen aspects of our deeper self and supporting us to become whole. This love is based in freedom, not expectation or need. Its wings take us higher and higher towards the universal love that experiences all as one.

THE LOVERS

✦   ✦   ✦

These three things are to be taken note of: the lowest love is sex – it is physical – and the highest refinement of love is compassion. Sex is below love, compassion is above love; love is exactly in the middle.

Very few people know what love is. Ninety-nine percent of people, unfortunately, think sexuality is love – it is not. Sexuality is very animal; it certainly has the potential of growing into love, but it is not actual love, only a potential....

If you become aware and alert, meditative, then sex can be transformed into love. And if your meditativeness becomes total, absolute, love can be transformed into compassion. Sex is the seed, love is the flower, compassion is the fragrance.

Buddha has defined compassion as 'love plus meditation'. When your love is not just a desire for the other, when your love is not only a need, when your love is a sharing, when your love is not that of a beggar but an emperor, when your love is not asking for something in return but is ready only to give – to give for the sheer joy of giving – then add meditation to it and the pure fragrance is released. That is compassion; compassion is the highest phenomenon.[7]

T he veil of illusion, or **maya**, *that has been keeping you from perceiving reality as it is, is starting to burn away. The fire is not the heated fire of passion, but the cool flame of awareness. As it burns the veil, the face of a very delicate and childlike buddha becomes visible.* ✦ *The awareness that is growing in you now is not the result of any conscious 'doing', nor do you need to struggle to make something happen. Any sense you might have had that you've been groping in the dark is dissolving now, or will be dissolving soon. Let yourself settle, and remember that deep inside you are just a witness, eternally silent, aware and unchanged. A channel is now opening from the circumference of activity to that center of witnessing. It will help you to become detached, and a new awareness will lift the veil from your eyes.*

AWARENESS

✦   ✦   ✦

MIND CAN NEVER BE INTELLIGENT – only no-mind is intelligent. Only no-mind is original and radical. Only no-mind is revolutionary – revolution in action.

This mind gives you a sort of stupor. Burdened by the memories of the past, burdened by the projections of the future, you go on living – at the minimum. You don't live at the maximum. Your flame remains very dim. Once you start dropping thoughts, the dust that you have collected in the past, the flame arises – clean, clear, alive, young. Your whole life becomes a flame, and a flame without any smoke. That is what awareness is.[8]

This card shows a small wildflower that has met the challenge of the rocks and stones in its path to emerge into the light of day. Surrounded by an aura of bright golden light, it exposes the majesty of its tiny self. Unashamed, it is equal to the brightest sun. ✦ When we are faced with a very difficult situation we have a choice: we can either be resentful, and try to find somebody or something to blame for the hardships, or we can face the challenge and grow. The flower shows us the way, as its passion for life leads it out of the darkness and into the light. There is no point fighting against the challenges of life, or trying to avoid or deny them. They are there, and if the seed is to become the flower we must go through them. Be courageous enough to grow into the flower you are meant to be.

COURAGE

✦   ✦   ✦

THE SEED CANNOT KNOW what is going to happen, the seed has never known the flower. And the seed cannot even believe that he has the potentiality to become a beautiful flower. Long is the journey, and it is always safer not to go on that journey because unknown is the path, nothing is guaranteed. Nothing can be guaranteed. Thousand and one are the hazards of the journey, many are the pitfalls – and the seed is secure, hidden inside a hard core. But the seed tries, it makes an effort; it drops the hard shell which is its security, it starts moving. Immediately the fight starts: the struggle with the soil, with the stones, with the rocks. And the seed was very hard and the sprout will be very, very soft and dangers will be many.-

There was no danger for the seed, the seed could have survived for millennia, but for the sprout many are the dangers. But the sprout starts towards the unknown, towards the sun, towards the source of light, not knowing where, not knowing why. Great is the cross to be carried, but a dream possesses the seed and the seed moves.

The same is the path for man. It is arduous. Much courage will be needed.[9]

When there is no 'significant other' in our lives we can either be lonely, or enjoy the freedom that solitude brings. When we find no support among others for our deeply felt truths, we can either feel isolated and bitter, or celebrate the fact that our vision is strong enough even to survive the powerful human need for the approval of family, friends or colleagues. If you are facing such a situation now, be aware of how you are choosing to view your 'aloneness' and take responsibility for the choice you have made. ◆ The humble figure in this card glows with a light that emanates from within. One of Gautam Buddha's most significant contributions to the spiritual life of humankind was to insist to his disciples, "Be a light unto yourself." Ultimately, each of us must develop within ourselves the capacity to make our way through the darkness without any companions, maps or guide.

ALONENESS

✦   ✦   ✦

WHEN YOU ARE ALONE you are not alone, you are simply lonely – and there is a tremendous difference between loneliness and aloneness. When you are lonely you are thinking of the other, you are missing the other. Loneliness is a negative state. You are feeling that it would have been better if the other was there – your friend, your wife, your mother, your beloved, your husband. It would have been good if the other was there, but the other is not.

Loneliness is absence of the other. Aloneness is the presence of oneself. Aloneness is very positive. It is a presence, overflowing presence. You are so full of presence that you can fill the whole universe with your presence and there is no need for anybody.[10]

The symbol in this card is an enormous wheel representing time, fate, karma. Galaxies spin around this constantly moving circle, and the twelve signs of the zodiac appear on its circumference. Just inside the circumference are the eight trigrams of the I Ching, and even closer to the center are the four directions, each illuminated by the energy of lightning. The spinning triangle is at this moment pointed upward, toward the divine, and the Chinese symbol of yin and yang, male and female, creative and receptive, lies at the center. ✦ It has often been said that the only unchanging thing in the world is change itself. Life is continuously changing, evolving, dying and being reborn. All opposites play a part in this vast circular pattern. If you cling to the edge of the wheel you can get dizzy! Move toward the center of the cyclone and relax, knowing that this too will pass.

CHANGE

✦ ✦ ✦

LIFE REPEATS ITSELF MINDLESSLY – unless you become mindful, it will go on repeating like a wheel. That's why Buddhists call it the wheel of life and death – the wheel of time. It moves like a wheel: birth is followed by death, death is followed by birth; love is followed by hate, hate is followed by love; success is followed by failure, failure is followed by success. Just see!

If you can watch just for a few days, you will see a pattern emerging, a wheel pattern. One day, a fine morning, you are feeling so good and so happy, and another day you are so dull, so dead that you start thinking of committing suicide. And just the other day you were so full of life, so blissful that you were feeling thankful to God that you were in a mood of deep gratefulness, and today there is great complaint and you don't see the point why one should go on living…. And it goes on and on, but you don't see the pattern.

Once you see the pattern, you can get out of it.[11]

The predominance of red in this card indicates at a glance that its subject is energy, power and strength. The brilliant glow emanates from the solar plexus, or center of power on the figure, and the posture is one of exuberance and determination. All of us occasionally reach a point when 'enough is enough'. At such times it seems we must do something, anything, even if it later turns out to be a mistake, to throw off the burdens and restrictions that are limiting us. If we don't, they threaten to suffocate and cripple our very life energy itself. ✦ If you are now feeling that 'enough is enough', allow yourself to take the risk of shattering the old patterns and limitations that have kept your energy from flowing. In doing so you will be amazed at the vitality and empowerment this Breakthrough can bring to your life.

BREAKTHROUGH

✦ ✦ ✦

To TRANSFORM BREAKDOWNS into breakthroughs is the whole function of a master. The psychotherapist simply patches you up. That is his function. He is not there to transform you. You need a metapsychology, the psychology of the buddhas.

It is the greatest adventure in life to go through a breakdown consciously. It is the greatest risk because there is no guarantee that the breakdown will become a breakthrough. It does become, but these things cannot be guaranteed. Your chaos is very ancient – for many, many lives you have been in chaos. It is thick and dense. It is almost a universe in itself. So when you enter into it with your small capacity, of course there is danger. But without facing this danger nobody has ever become integrated, nobody has ever become an individual, indivisible.

Zen, or meditation, is the method which will help you to go through the chaos, through the dark night of the soul, balanced, disciplined, alert.

The dawn is not far away, but before you can reach the dawn, the dark night has to be passed through. And as the dawn comes closer, the night will become darker.[12]

*T*he figure on this card is being born anew, emerging from his earthbound roots and growing wings to fly into the unbounded. The geometric shapes around the body of the figure show the many dimensions of life simultaneously available to him. The square represents the physical, the manifest, the known. The circle represents the unmanifest, the spirit, pure space. And the triangle symbolizes the threefold nature of the universe: manifest, unmanifest, and the human being who contains both. ✦ Now you are presented with an opportunity to see life in all its dimensions, from the depths to the heights. They exist together, and when we come to know from experience that the dark and the difficult are needed as much as the light and easy, then we begin to have a very different perspective on the world. By allowing all of life's colors to penetrate us, we become more integrated.

NEW VISION

✦ ✦ ✦

WHEN YOU OPEN UP to the ultimate, immediately it pours into you. You are no longer an ordinary human being – you have transcended. Your insight has become the insight of the whole existence. Now you are no longer separate – you have found your roots. Otherwise, ordinarily, everybody is moving without roots, not knowing from where their heart goes on receiving energy, not knowing who goes on breathing in them, not knowing the life juice that is running inside them.

It is not the body, it is not the mind – it is something transcendental to all duality, that is called *bhagavat – the bhagavat in the ten directions* ....

Your inner being, when it opens, first experiences two directions: the height, the depth. And then slowly, slowly, as this becomes your established situation, you start looking around, spreading into all other eight directions.

And once you have attained to the point where your height and your depth meet, then you can look around to the very circumference of the universe. Then your consciousness starts unfolding in all ten directions, but the road has been one. [13]

The central figure in this card sits atop the vast flower of the void, and holds the symbols of transformation – the sword that cuts through illusion, the snake that rejuvenates itself by shedding its skin, the broken chain of limitations, and the yin/yang symbol of transcending duality. One of its hands rests on its lap, open and receptive. The other reaches down to touch the mouth of a sleeping face, symbolizing the silence that comes when we are at rest. ✦ This is a time for a deep let-go. Allow any pain, sorrow, or difficulty just to be there, accepting its 'facticity'. It is very much like the experience of Gautam Buddha when, after years of seeking, he finally gave up knowing there was nothing more that he could do. That very night, he became enlightened. Transformation comes, like death, in its own time. And, like death, it takes you from one dimension into another.

TRANSFORMATION

✦　✦　✦

A MASTER IN ZEN is not simply a teacher. In all the religions there are only teachers. They teach you about subjects which you don't know, and they ask you to believe, because there is no way to bring those experiences into objective reality. Neither has the teacher known them – he has believed them; he transfers his belief to somebody else. Zen is not a believer's world. It is not for the faithful ones; it is for those daring souls who can drop all belief, unbelief, doubt, reason, mind, and simply enter into their pure existence without boundaries.

But it brings a tremendous transformation. Hence, let me say that while others are involved in philosophies, Zen is involved in metamorphosis, in a transformation. It is authentic alchemy: it changes you from base metal into gold. But its language has to be understood, not with your reasoning and intellectual mind but with your loving heart. Or even just listening, not bothering whether it is true or not. And a moment comes suddenly that you see it, which has been eluding you your whole life. Suddenly, what Gautam Buddha called 'eighty-four thousand doors' open.[14]

The image of integration is the unio mystica, the fusion of opposites. This is a time of communication between the previously experienced dualities of life. Rather than night opposing day, dark suppressing light, they work together to create a unified whole, turning endlessly one into the other, each containing in its deepest core the seed of the opposite.

✦ The eagle and the swan are both beings of flight and majesty. The eagle is the embodiment of power and aloneness. The swan is the embodiment of space and purity, gently floating and diving upon and within the element of the emotions, entirely content and complete within her perfection and beauty.

✦ We are the union of eagle and swan: male and female, fire and water, life and death. The card of integration is the symbol of self-creation, new life, and mystical union; otherwise known as alchemy.

INTEGRATION

✦　　✦　　✦

THE CONFLICT IS IN MAN. Unless it is resolved there, it cannot be resolved anywhere else. The politics is within you; it is between the two parts of the mind.

A very small bridge exists. If that bridge is broken through some accident, through some physiological defect or something else, the person becomes split, the person becomes two persons – and the phenomenon of schizophrenia or split personality happens. If the bridge is broken – and the bridge is very fragile – then you become two, you behave like two persons. In the morning you are very loving, very beautiful; in the evening you are very angry, absolutely different. You don't remember your morning…how can you remember? Another mind was functioning – and the person becomes two persons. If this bridge is strengthened so much that the two minds disappear as two and become one, then integration, then crystallization, arises. What George Gurdjieff used to call the crystallization of being is nothing but these two minds becoming one, the meeting of the male and the female within, the meeting of yin and yang, the meeting of the left and right, the meeting of logic and illogic, the meeting of Plato and Aristotle.[15]

This card recalls an old Zen story, about a lion who was brought up by sheep and who thought he was a sheep until an old lion captured him and took him to a pond, where he showed him his own reflection. Many of us are like this lion – the image we have of ourselves comes not from our own direct experience but from the opinions of others. A 'personality' imposed from the outside replaces the individuality that could have grown from within. We become just another sheep in the herd, unable to move freely, and unconscious of our own true identity. ✦ It's time to take a look at your own reflection in the pond, and make a move to break out of whatever you have been conditioned by others to believe about yourself. Dance, run, jog, do gibberish – whatever is needed to wake up the sleeping lion within.

CONDITIONING

✦   ✦   ✦

UNLESS YOU DROP your personality you will not be able to find your individuality. Individuality is given by existence; personality is imposed by the society. Personality is social convenience.

Society cannot tolerate individuality, because individuality will not follow like a sheep. Individuality has the quality of the lion; the lion moves alone.

The sheep are always in the crowd, hoping that being in the crowd will feel cozy. Being in the crowd one feels more protected, secure. If somebody attacks, there is every possibility in a crowd to save yourself. But alone? – only the lions move alone.

And every one of you is born a lion, but the society goes on conditioning you, programming your mind as a sheep. It gives you a personality, a cozy personality, nice, very convenient, very obedient.

Society wants slaves, not people who are absolutely dedicated to freedom. Society wants slaves because all the vested interests want obedience.[16]

The card shows a tower being burned, destroyed, blown apart. A man and a woman are leaping from it not because they want to, but because they have no choice. In the background is a transparent, meditating figure representing the witnessing consciousness. ✦ You might be feeling pretty shaky right now, as if the earth is rocking beneath your feet. Your sense of security is being challenged, and the natural tendency is to try to hold on to whatever you can. But this inner earthquake is both necessary and tremendously important — if you allow it, you will emerge from the wreckage stronger and more available for new experiences. After the fire, the earth is replenished; after the storm the air is clear. Try to watch the destruction with detachment, almost as if it were happening to somebody else. Say yes to the process by meeting it halfway.

THUNDERBOLT

✦ ✦ ✦

What meditation does slowly, slowly, a good shout of the master, unexpectedly, in the situation where the disciple was asking some question, and the master jumps and shouts, or hits him, or throws him out of the door, or jumps over him…. These methods were never known. It was purely the very creative genius of Ma Tzu, and he made many people enlightened.

Sometimes it looks so hilarious: he threw a man from the window, from a two-storey house, and the man had come to ask on what to meditate. And Ma Tzu not only threw him, he jumped after him, fell on him, sat on his chest, and he said, "Got it?!"

And the poor fellow said, "Yes" – because if you say "No," he may beat you or do something else. It is enough – his body is fractured, and Ma Tzu, sitting on his chest, says, "Got it?!"

And in fact he got it, because it was so sudden, out of the blue – he could never have conceived it.[17]

The silent mirrorlike receptiveness of a star-filled night with a full moon is reflected in the misty lake below. The face in the sky is deep in meditation, a goddess of the night who brings depth, peace and understanding. ✦ Now is a very precious time. It will be easy for you to rest inside, to plumb the depths of your own inner silence to the point where it meets the silence of the universe. ✦ There's nothing to do, nowhere to go, and the quality of your inner silence permeates everything you do. It might make some people uncomfortable, accustomed as they are to all the noise and activity of the world. Never mind; seek out those who can resonate with your silence, or enjoy your aloneness. Now is the time to come home to yourself. The understanding and insights that come to you in these moments will be manifested later on, in a more outgoing phase of your life.

SILENCE

✦ ✦ ✦

THE ENERGY OF THE WHOLE has taken possession of you. You are possessed, you are no more, the whole is. This moment, as the silence penetrates in you, you can understand the significance of it, because it is the same silence that Gautam Buddha experienced. It is the same silence that Chuang Tzu or Bodhidharma or Nansen.... The taste of the silence is the same.

Time changes, the world goes on changing, but the experience of silence, the joy of it, remains the same. That is the only thing you can rely upon, the only thing that never dies. It is the only thing that you can call your very being.[18]

The hands of existence form the shape of the female genitals, the opening of the cosmic mother. Revealed within are many images, faces from other times. While it might be entertaining to fantasize about famous past lives, it is just a distraction. The real point is to see and understand the karmic patterns of our lives, and their roots in an endless repetitive cycle that traps us in unconscious behavior. ✦ The two rainbow lizards on either side represent knowing and not-knowing. They are the guardians of the unconscious, making sure that we are prepared for a vision that might otherwise be shattering. A glimpse into the eternity of our existence is a gift, and understanding the function of karma in our lives is not something that can be grasped at will. This is a wake-up call; the events in your life are trying to show you a pattern as ancient as the journey of your own soul.

PAST LIVES

✦   ✦   ✦

THE CHILD CAN BECOME CONSCIOUS only if in his past life he has meditated enough, has created enough meditative energy to fight with the darkness that death brings. One simply is lost in an oblivion and then suddenly finds a new womb and forgets completely about the old body. There is a discontinuity. This darkness, this unconsciousness creates the discontinuity.

The East has been working hard to penetrate these barriers. And ten thousand years' work has not been in vain. Everybody can penetrate to the past life or many past lives. But for that you have to go deeper into your meditation, for two reasons: unless you go deeper, you cannot find the door to another life; secondly, you have to be deeper in meditation because, if you find the door of another life, a flood of events will come into the mind.

It is hard enough even to carry one life....[19]

The old man in this card radiates a childlike delight in the world. There is a sense of grace surrounding him, as if he is at home with himself and with what life has brought. He seems to be having a playful communication with the praying mantis on his finger, as if the two of them are the greatest friends. The pink flowers cascading around him represent a time of letting go, relaxation and sweetness. They are a response to his presence, a reflection of his own qualities. ✦ The innocence that comes from a deep experience of life is childlike, but not childish. The innocence of children is beautiful, but ignorant. It will be replaced by mistrust and doubt as the child grows and learns that the world can be a dangerous and threatening place. But the innocence of a life lived fully has a quality of wisdom and acceptance of the ever-changing wonder of life.

INNOCENCE

✦   ✦   ✦

ZEN SAYS THAT IF YOU DROP KNOWLEDGE – and within knowledge everything is included, your name, your identity, everything, because this has been given to you by others – if you drop all that has been given by others, you will have a totally different quality to your being – innocence.

This will be a crucifixion of the persona, the personality, and there will be a resurrection of your innocence; you will become a child again, reborn.[20]

The butterfly in this card represents the outer, that which is constantly moving and that which is not real but an illusion. Behind the butterfly is the face of consciousness, looking inward to that which is eternal. The space between the two eyes has opened, revealing the lotus of spiritual unfoldment and the rising sun of awareness. Through the rising of the inner sun, meditation is born. ◆ The card reminds us not to look outside for what is real, but to look within. When we focus on externals, we too often get caught up in judgments — this is good, this is bad, I want this, I don't want that. These judgments keep us trapped in our illusions, our sleepiness, our old habits and patterns. Drop your opinionated mind, and move inside. There, you can relax into your own deepest truth, where the difference between dreams and reality is already known.

BEYOND ILLUSION

◆   ◆   ◆

THIS IS THE ONLY DISTINCTION between the dream and the real: reality allows you to doubt, and the dream does not allow you to doubt....

To me, the capacity to doubt is one of the greatest blessings to humanity. The religions have been enemies because they have been cutting the very roots of doubt, and there is a reason why they have been doing that: because they want people to believe in certain illusions that they have been preaching....

Why have the people like Gautam Buddha been so insistent that the whole existence – except your witnessing self, except your awareness – is just ephemeral, made of the same stuff as dreams are made of? They are not saying that these trees are not there. They are not saying that these pillars are not there. Don't misunderstand because of the word 'illusion'.... It has been translated as illusion, but illusion is not the right word. Illusion does not exist. Reality exists. Maya is just in between – it almost exists. As far as day-to-day activities are concerned, it can be taken as reality. Only in the ultimate sense, from the peak of your illumination, it becomes unreal, illusory.[21]

Here the last piece of a jigsaw puzzle is being put into its place, the position of the third eye, the place of inner perception. Even in the ever-changing flow of life there are moments in which we come to a point of completion. In these moments we are able to perceive the whole picture, the composite of all the small pieces that have occupied our attention for so long. In the finishing, we can either be in despair because we don't want the situation to come to an end, or we can be grateful and accepting of the fact that life is full of endings and new beginnings. ✦ Whatever has been absorbing your time and energy is now coming to an end. In completing it, you will be clearing the space for something new to begin. Use this interval to celebrate both — the end of the old and the coming of the new.

COMPLETION

✦   ✦   ✦

THIS IS THE WAY OF ZEN, not to say things to their completion. This has to be understood; it is a very important methodology. Not to say everything means to give an opportunity to the listener to complete it. All answers are incomplete. The master has only given you a direction... By the time you reach the limit, you will know what is going to remain.

This way, if somebody is trying to understand Zen intellectually he will fail. It is not an answer to the question but something more than the answer. It is indicating the very reality.... The buddha nature is not something far away – your very consciousness is buddha nature. And your consciousness can witness these things which constitute the world. The world will end but the mirror will remain, mirroring nothing.[22]

The Master in Zen is not a master over others, but a master of himself. His every gesture and his every word reflect his enlightened state. He has no private goals, no desire that anything should be other than the way it is. His disciples gather around him not to follow him, but to soak up his presence and be inspired by his example. In his eyes they find their own truth reflected, and in his silence they fall more easily into the silence of their own beings. The master welcomes the disciples not because he wants to lead them, but because he has so much to share. Together, they create an energy field that supports each unique individual in finding his or her own light. ✦ *If you can find such a master you are blessed. If you cannot, keep on searching. Learn from the teachers, and the would-be masters, and move on.* Charaiveti, charaiveti, *said Gautam Buddha. Keep on moving.*

THE MASTER

✦ ✦ ✦

BEYOND MIND, there is an awareness that is intrinsic, that is not given to you by the outside, and is not an idea – and there is no experiment up to now that has found any center in the brain which corresponds to awareness. The whole work of meditation is to make you aware of all that is "mind" and disidentify yourself from it. That very separation is the greatest revolution that can happen to man.

Now you can do and act on only that which makes you more joyous, fulfills you, gives you contentment, makes your life a work of art, a beauty. But this is possible only if the master in you is awake. Right now the master is fast asleep. And the mind, the servant, is playing the role of master. And the servant is not even *your* servant; the servant is created by the outside world, it follows the outside world and its laws.

Once your awareness becomes a flame, it burns up the whole slavery that the mind has created. There is no blissfulness more precious than freedom, than being a master of your own destiny.[23]

The Zen master in this card has harnessed the energy of fire and is able to use it for creation rather than destruction. He invites us to recognize and participate with him in the understanding that belongs to those who have mastered the fires of passion, without repressing them or allowing them to get destructive and out of balance. He is so integrated that there is no longer any difference between who he is inside and who he is in the world outside. He offers this gift of understanding and integration to all those who come to him, the gift of creative light that comes from the center of his being. ✦ The King of Fire tells us that anything that we undertake now, with the understanding that comes from maturity, will bring enrichment to our own lives and to the lives of others. Using whatever skills you have, whatever you have learned from your own life experience, it is time to express yourself.

THE CREATOR

✦ ✦ ✦

THERE ARE TWO TYPES of creators in the world: one type of creator works with objects – a poet, a painter, they work with objects, they create things; the other type of creator, the mystic, creates himself. He doesn't work with objects, he works with the subject; he works on himself, his own being. And he is the real creator, the real poet because he makes himself into a masterpiece.

You are carrying a masterpiece hidden within you, but you are standing in the way. Just move aside, then the masterpiece will be revealed. Everyone is a masterpiece, because God never gives birth to anything less than that. Everyone carries that masterpiece hidden for many lives, not knowing who they are, and just trying on the surface to become someone.

Drop the idea of becoming someone, because you already are a masterpiece. You cannot be improved. You have only to come to it, to know it, to realize it. God has himself created you, you cannot be improved.[24]

The Queen of Fire is so rich, so much a queen, that she can afford to give. It doesn't even occur to her to take inventories or to put something aside for later. She dispenses her treasures without limits, welcoming all and sundry to partake of the abundance, fertility and light that surrounds her. ✦ When you draw this card, it suggests that you too are in a situation where you have an opportunity to share your love, your joy and your laughter. And in sharing, you find that you feel even more full. There is no need to go anywhere or to make any special effort. You find that you can enjoy sensuality without possessiveness or attachment, can give birth to a child or to a new project with an equal sense of creativity fulfilled. Everything around you seems to be 'coming together' now. Enjoy it, ground yourself in it, and let the abundance in you and around you overflow.

SHARING

✦   ✦   ✦

A S YOU MOVE ABOVE to the fourth center – that is the heart – your whole life becomes a sharing of love. The third center has created the abundance of love. By reaching to the third center in meditation, you have become so overflowing with love, with compassion, and you want to share. It happens at the fourth center – the heart.

That's why even in the ordinary world people think love comes out of the heart. For them it is just hearsay, they have heard it; they don't know it because they have never reached to their heart. But the meditator finally reaches to the heart. As he has reached to the center of his being – the third center – suddenly an explosion of love and compassion and joy and blissfulness and benediction has arisen in him with such a force that it hits his heart and opens the heart. The heart is just in the middle of all your seven centers – three centers below, three centers above. You have come exactly to the middle.[25]

The figure in this card has taken on the shape of an arrow, moving with the single-pointed focus of one who knows precisely where he is going. He is moving so fast that he has become almost pure energy. But his intensity should not be mistaken for the manic energy that makes people drive their cars at top speed to get from point A to point B. That kind of intensity belongs to the horizontal world of space and time. The intensity represented by the Knight of Fire belongs to the vertical world of the present moment — a recognition that now is the only moment there is, and here is the only space. ✦ When you act with the intensity of the Knight of Fire it is likely to create ripples in the waters around you. Some will feel uplifted and refreshed by your presence, others may feel threatened or annoyed. But the opinions of others matter little; nothing can hold you back right now.

INTENSITY

✦ ✦ ✦

ZEN SAYS: Think of all the great words and great teachings as your deadly enemy. Avoid them, because you have to find your own source.

You have not to be a follower, an imitator. You have to be an original individual; you have to find your innermost core on your own, with no guide, no guiding scriptures. It is a dark night, but with the intense fire of inquiry you are bound to come to the sunrise. Everybody who has burned with intense inquiry has found the sunrise. Others only believe. Those who believe are not religious, they are simply avoiding the great adventure of religion by believing.[26]

L ife is rarely as serious as we believe it to be, and when we recognize this fact, it responds by giving us more and more opportunities to play. The woman in this card is celebrating the joy of being alive, like a butterfly that has emerged from its chrysalis into the promise of the light. She reminds us of the time when we were children, discovering seashells on the beach or building castles in the sand without any concern that the waves might come and wash them away in the next moment. She knows that life is a game, and she's playing the part of a clown right now with no sense of embarrassment or pretense. ✦ When the Page of Fire enters your life, it is a sign that you are ready for the fresh and the new. Something wonderful is just on the horizon, and you have just the right quality of playful innocence and clarity to welcome it with open arms.

*P*LAYFULNESS

✦   ✦   ✦

THE MOMENT YOU START seeing life as non-serious, a playfulness, all the burden on your heart disappears. All the fear of death, of life, of love – everything disappears. One starts living with a very light weight or almost no weight. So weightless one becomes, one can fly in the open sky.

Zen's greatest contribution is to give you an alternative to the serious man.

The serious man has made the world, the serious man has made all the religions. He has created all the philosophies, all the cultures, all the moralities; everything that exists around you is a creation of the serious man.

Zen has dropped out of the serious world. It has created a world of its own which is very playful, full of laughter, where even great masters behave like children.[27]

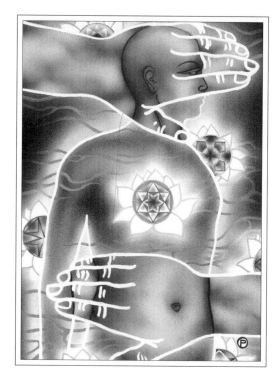

It is a time when the deeply buried wounds of the past are coming to the surface, ready and available to be healed. The figure in this card is naked, vulnerable, open to the loving touch of existence. The aura around his body is full of light, and the quality of relaxation, caring and love that surrounds him is dissolving his struggle and suffering. Lotuses of light appear on his physical body, and around the subtle energy bodies that healers say surround each of us. In each of these subtle layers appears a healing crystal or pattern. ✦ When we are under the healing influence of the King of Water we are no longer hiding from ourselves or others. In this attitude of openness and acceptance we can be healed, and help others also to be healthy and whole.

HEALING

✦   ✦   ✦

NO, YOU CARRY YOUR WOUND. With the ego your whole being is a wound. And you carry it around. Nobody is interested in hurting you, nobody is positively waiting to hurt you; everybody is engaged in safeguarding his own wound. Who has got the energy? But still it happens, because you are so ready to be wounded, so ready, just waiting on the brink for anything.

You cannot touch a man of Tao. Why? – because there is no one to be touched. There is no wound. He is healthy, healed, whole. This word 'whole' is beautiful. The word 'heal' comes from the whole, and the word 'holy' also comes from the whole. He is whole, healed, holy.

Be aware of your wound. Don't help it to grow, let it be healed; and it will be healed only when you move to the roots. The less the head, the more the wound will heal; with no head there is no wound. Live a headless life. Move as a total being, and accept things. Just for twenty-four hours, try it – total acceptance, whatsoever happens. Someone insults you, accept it, don't react, and see what happens. Suddenly you will feel an energy flowing in you that you have not felt before.[28]

Receptivity represents the feminine, receptive quality of water and of the emotions. Her arms are extended upwards to receive, and she is completely immersed in the water. She has no head, no busy and aggressive mind to hinder her pure receptivity. And as she is filled she is continuously emptying herself, overflowing, and receiving more. The lotus pattern or matrix that emerges from her represents the perfect harmony of the universe that becomes apparent when we are in tune with it. ✦ The Queen of Water brings a time of unboundedness and gratitude for whatever life brings, without any expectations or demands. Neither duty or thought of merit or reward are important. Sensitivity, intuition and compassion are the qualities that shine forth now, dissolving all the obstacles that keep us separate from each other and from the whole.

RECEPTIVITY

✦ ✦ ✦

Listening is one of the basic secrets of entering into the temple of God. Listening means passivity. Listening means forgetting yourself completely – only then can you listen. When you listen attentively to somebody, you forget yourself. If you cannot forget yourself, you never listen. If you are too self-conscious about yourself, you simply pretend that you are listening – you don't listen. You may nod your head; you may sometimes say yes and no – but you are not listening.

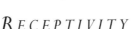

When you listen you become just a passage, a passivity, a receptivity, a womb: you become feminine. And to arrive one has to become feminine. You cannot reach God as aggressive invaders, conquerors. You can reach God only…or it will be better to say; God can reach you only when you are receptive, a feminine receptivity. When you become *yin*, a receptivity, the door is open. And you wait.

Listening is the art for becoming passive.[29]

N ow is the moment to be a bungee jumper without the cord! And it is this quality of absolute trust, with no reservations or secret safety nets, that the Knight of Water demands from us. There is a tremendous sense of exhilaration if we can take the jump and move into the unknown, even if the idea scares us to death. And when we take trust to the level of the quantum leap, we don't make any elaborate plans or preparations. We don't say, "Okay, I trust that I know what to do now, and I'll settle my things and pack my suitcase and take it with me." No, we just jump, with hardly a thought for what happens next. ✦ The leap is the thing, and the thrill of it as we free-fall through the empty sky. The card gives a hint here, though, about what waits for us at the other end — a soft, welcoming, yummy pink, rose petals, juicy...c'mon!

TRUST

❖   ❖   ❖

DON'T WASTE your life for that which is going to be taken away. Trust life. If you trust, only then can you drop your knowledge, only then can you put your mind aside. And with trust, something immense opens up. Then this life is no longer ordinary life, it becomes full of God, overflowing. When the heart is innocent and the walls have disappeared, you are bridged with infinity. And you are not deceived; there is nothing that can be taken away from you. That which can be taken away from you is not worth keeping, and that which cannot be taken away from you, why should one be afraid of its being taken away? – it cannot be taken away, there is no possibility. You cannot lose your real treasure.[30]

The bird pictured on this card is looking out from what seems to be a cage. There is no door, and actually the bars are disappearing. The bars were an illusion, and this small bird is being summoned by the grace and freedom and encouragement of the others. It is spreading its wings, ready to take flight for the very first time. ✦ The dawn of a new understanding – that the cage has always been open, and the sky has always been there for us to explore – can make us feel a little shaky at first. It's fine, and natural to be shaky, but don't let it overshadow the opportunity to experience the light-heartedness and adventure on offer, right there alongside the shakiness. Move with the sweetness and gentleness of this time. Feel the fluttering within. Spread your wings and be free.

UNDERSTANDING

✦ ✦ ✦

YOU ARE OUT OF jail, out of the cage; you can open your wings and the whole sky is yours. All the stars and the moon and the sun belong to you. You can disappear into the blueness of the beyond…. Just drop clinging to this cage, move out of the cage and the whole sky is yours.

Open your wings and fly across the sun like an eagle. In the inner sky, in the inner world, freedom is the highest value – everything else is secondary, even blissfulness, ecstasy. There are thousands of flowers, uncountable, but they all become possible in the climate of freedom.[31]

There is a time and a place for control, but if we put it in charge of our lives we end up totally rigid. The figure is encased in the angles of pyramid shapes that surround him. Light glitters and glints off his shiny surfaces, but does not penetrate. It's as if he is almost mummified inside this structure he's built up around himself. His fists are clenched, and his stare is blank, almost blind. The lower part of his body beneath the table is a knife point, a cutting edge that divides and separates. His world is ordered and perfect, but it is not alive – he cannot allow any spontaneity or vulnerability to enter it. ◆ The image of the King of Clouds reminds us to take a deep breath, loosen our neckties and take it easy. If mistakes happen, it's okay. If things get a little out of hand, it's probably just what the doctor ordered. There is much, much more to life than being 'on top of things'.

CONTROL

✦ ✦ ✦

CONTROLLED PERSONS are always nervous because deep down turmoil is still hidden. If you are uncontrolled, flowing, alive, then you are not nervous. There is no question of being nervous – whatsoever happens, happens. You have no expectations for the future, you are not performing. Then why should you be nervous?

To control that mind one has to remain so cold and frozen that no life energy is allowed to move into your limbs, into your body. If energy is allowed to move, those repressions will surface. That's why people have learned how to be cold, how to touch others and yet not touch them, how to see people and yet not see them. People live with clichés – "Hallo. How are you?" Nobody means anything. These are just to avoid the real encounter of two persons. People don't look into each other's eyes, they don't hold hands, they don't try to feel each other's energy, they don't allow each other to pour – very afraid, somehow just managing, cold and dead, in a straitjacket.[32]

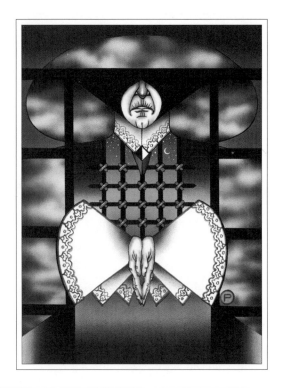

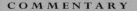

Morality has restricted all the juice and energy of life to the narrow confines of her mind. It can't flow there, so she really has become 'a dried up old prune'. Her whole manner is very proper and stiff and severe, and she is always ready to see every situation as black and white, like the jewel she wears around her neck. ✦ The Queen of Clouds lurks in the minds of all of us who have been brought up with rigid ideas of good and bad, sinful and virtuous, acceptable and unacceptable, moral and immoral. It's important to remember that all these judgments of the mind are just products of our conditioning. And whether our judgments are applied to ourselves or to others, they keep us from experiencing the beauty and godliness that lies within. Only when we break through the cage of our conditioning and reach the truth of our own hearts can we begin to see life as it really is.

MORALITY

✦   ✦   ✦

ODHIDHARMA ... far transcends moralists, puritans, so-called good people, do-gooders. He has touched the very rock bottom of the problem.

Unless awareness arises in you, all your morality is bogus, all your culture is simply a thin layer which can be destroyed by anybody. But once your morality has come out of your awareness, not out of a certain discipline, then it is a totally different matter. Then you will respond in every situation out of your awareness. And whatever you do will be good. Awareness cannot do anything that is bad. That is the ultimate beauty of awareness, that anything that comes out of it is simply beautiful, is simply right, and without any effort and without any practice.

So rather than cutting the leaves and the branches, cut the root. And to cut the root there is no other method than a single method: the method of being alert, of being aware, of being conscious.[33]

*T*he figure in this card is completely covered in armor. Only his glare of rage is visible, and the whites of the knuckles on his clenched fists. If you look closely at the armor, you can see it's covered with buttons, ready to detonate if anybody so much as brushes up against them. In the background we see the shadowy movie that plays in this man's mind — two figures fighting for a castle. ✦ An explosive temper or a smoldering rage often masks a deep feeling of pain. We think that if we frighten people away, we can avoid being hurt even more. In fact, just the opposite is the case. By covering our wounds with armor we are preventing them from being healed. By lashing out at others we keep ourselves from getting the love and nourishment we need. If this description seems to fit you, it's time to stop fighting. There is so much love available to you if you just let it in. Start by forgiving yourself: you're worth it.

FIGHTING

✦ ✦ ✦

ONE MOMENT IT WAS THERE, another moment it is gone. One moment we are here, and another moment we have gone. And for this simple moment, how much fuss we make – how much violence, ambition, struggle, conflict, anger, hatred.

Just for this small moment! Just waiting for the train in a waiting room on a station, and creating so much fuss: fighting, hurting each other, trying to possess, trying to boss, trying to dominate – all that politics. And then the train comes and you are gone forever.[34]

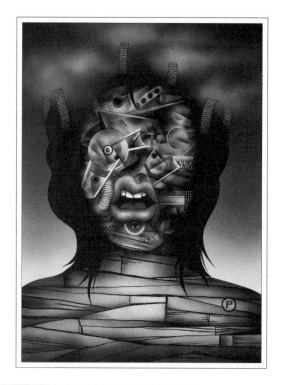

This is what happens when we forget that the mind is meant to be a servant, and start to allow it to run our lives. The head is filled with mechanisms, the mouth is ranting and raving, and the whole surrounding atmosphere is being polluted by this factory of arguments and opinions. "But wait," you say. "The mind is what makes us human, it's the source of all progress, all great truths." If you believe that, try an experiment: go into your room, shut the door, turn on a tape recorder, and give yourself total permission to say whatever is 'on your mind'. If you really allow it to all come out without any censorship or editing, you'll be amazed at the amount of rubbish that comes spewing forth. ✦ The Page of Clouds is telling you that somebody, somewhere, is stuck in 'a head trip'. Take a look and make sure it isn't you.

MIND

✦   ✦   ✦

THIS IS THE SITUATION of your head: I see cycle-handles and pedals and strange things that you have gathered from everywhere. Such a small head…and no space to live in! And that rubbish goes on moving in your head; your head goes on spinning and weaving – it keeps you occupied. Just think what kind of thoughts go on inside your mind.

One day just sit, close your doors, and write down for half an hour whatsoever is

passing in your mind, and you will understand what I mean and you will be surprised what goes on inside your mind. It remains in the background, it is constantly there, it surrounds you like a cloud. With this cloud you cannot know reality; you cannot attain to spiritual perception. This cloud has to be dropped. And it is just with your decision to drop it that it will disappear. You are clinging to it – the cloud is not interested in you, remember it. [35]

This Dionysian character is the very picture of a whole man, a 'Zorba the Buddha' who can drink wine, dance on the beach and sing in the rain, and at the same time enjoy the depths of understanding and wisdom that belong to the sage. In one hand he holds a lotus, showing that he respects and contains within himself the grace of the feminine. His exposed chest (an open heart) and relaxed belly show that he is at home with his masculinity as well, utterly self-contained. The four elements of earth, fire, water and sky all conjunct at the King of Rainbows who sits atop the book of the wisdom of life.

✦ If you are a woman, the King of Rainbows brings the support of your own male energies into your life, a union with the soulmate within. For a man, this card represents a time of breaking through the conventional male stereotypes and allowing the fullness of the whole human being to shine forth.

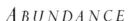
ABUNDANCE

✦   ✦   ✦

IN THE EAST people have condemned the body, condemned matter, called matter 'illusory', maya – it does not really exist, it only appears to exist; it is made of the same stuff as dreams are made of. They denied the world, and that is the reason for the East remaining poor, sick, in starvation.

Half of humanity has been accepting the inner world but denying the outer world. The other half of humanity has been accepting the material world and denying the inner world. Both are half, and no man who is half can be contented.

You have to be whole: rich in the body, rich in science; rich in meditation, rich in consciousness. Only a whole person is a holy person, according to me.

I want Zorba and Buddha to meet together. Zorba alone is hollow. His dance has not an eternal significance, it is momentary pleasure. Soon he will be tired of it. Unless you have inexhaustible sources, available to you from the cosmos itself…unless you become existential, you cannot become whole.

This is my contribution to humanity: the whole person.[36]

The Queen of Rainbows is like a fantastic plant that has reached the apex of its flowering and its colors. She is very sexual, very alive, and full of possibilities. She snaps her fingers to the music of love, and her zodiac necklace is placed in a way that Venus lies over her heart. The sleeves of her garment contain an abundance of seeds, and as the wind blows the seeds will be scattered to take root where they may. She is not concerned whether they land on the soil or on the rocks — she is just spreading them everywhere in sheer celebration of life and love. Flowers fall on her from above, in harmony with her own flowering, and the waters of emotion swirl playfully beneath the flower on which she sits. ✦ You might feel like a garden of flowers right now, showered with blessings from everywhere. Welcome the bees, invite the birds to drink your nectar. Spread your joy around for all to share.

FLOWERING

✦ ✦ ✦

ZEN WANTS YOU LIVING, living in abundance, living in totality, living intensely – not at the minimum as Christianity wants you, but at the maximum, over-flowing. Your life should reach to others. Your blissfulness, your benediction, your ecstasy should not be contained within you like a seed. It should open like a flower and spread its fragrance to all and sundry – not only to the friends but to the strangers too.

This is real compassion, this is real love: sharing your enlightenment, sharing your dance of the beyond.[37]

The Knight of Rainbows is a reminder that, just like this tortoise, we carry our home with us wherever we go. There is no need to hurry, no need to seek shelter elsewhere. Even as we move into the depths of the emotional waters, we can remain self-contained and free from attachments. ✦ It is a time when you are ready to let go of any expectations you have had about yourself or other people, and to take responsibility for any illusions you might have been carrying. There is no need to do anything but rest in the fullness of who you are right now. If desires and hopes and dreams are fading away, so much the better. Their disappearance is making space for a new quality of stillness and acceptance of what is, and you are able to welcome this development in a way you have never been able to before. Savor this quality of slowing down, of coming to rest and recognizing that you are already at home.

SLOWING DOWN

✦ ✦ ✦

MEDITATION IS A KIND OF MEDICINE — its use is only for the time being. Once you have learned the quality, then you need not do any particular meditation, then the meditation has to spread all over your life.

Walking is Zen, sitting is Zen.

Then what will be the quality? Watchfully, alert, joyously, unmotivated, centered, loving, flowing, one walks. And the walking is sauntering. Loving, alert, watchful, one sits, unmotivated — not sitting for anything in particular, just enjoying how beautiful just sitting doing nothing is, how relaxing, how restful....

After a long walk, you sit under a tree and the breeze comes and cools you. Each moment one has to be at ease with oneself — not trying to improve, not cultivating anything, not practicing anything.

Walking is Zen, sitting is Zen,
Talking or silent, moving, unmoving,
The essence is at ease.

The essence is at ease: that is the keyword. *The essence is at ease:* that is the key statement. Do whatsoever you are doing, but at the deepest core remain at ease, cool, calm, centered.[38]

When we are truly in a spirit of adventure, we are moving just like this child. Full of trust, out of the darkness of the forest into the rainbow of the light, we go step by step, drawn by our sense of wonder into the unknown. ✦ Adventure really has nothing to do with plans and maps and programs and organization. The Page of Rainbows represents a quality that can come to us anywhere — at home or in the office, in the wilderness or in the city, in a creative project or in our relationships with others. Whenever we move into the new and unknown with the trusting spirit of a child, innocent and open and vulnerable, even the smallest things of life can become the greatest adventures.

ADVENTURE

✦ ✦ ✦

ZEN SAYS truth has nothing to do with authority, truth has nothing to do with tradition, truth has nothing to do with the past – truth is a radical, personal realization. You have to come to it.

Knowledge is certain; the search for personal knowing is very, very hazardous. Nobody can guarantee it. If you ask me if I can guarantee anything, I say I cannot guarantee you anything. I can only guarantee danger, that much is certain. I can only guarantee you a long adventure with every possibility of going astray and never reaching the goal. But one thing is certain: the very search will help you to grow. I can guarantee only growth. Danger will be there, sacrifice will be there; you will be moving every day into the unknown, into the uncharted, and there will be no map to follow, no guide to follow. Yes, there are millions of dangers and you can go astray and you can get lost, but that is the only way one grows. Insecurity is the only way to grow, to face danger is the only way to grow, to accept the challenge of the unknown is the only way to grow.[39]

T he eagle has an overview of all the possibilities contained in the landscape below, as he flies freely, naturally and effortlessly through the sky. He is really in his domain, very grand and self-contained. ✦ This card indicates that you are at a point where a world of possibilities is open to you. Because you have grown more loving towards yourself, more self-contained, you can work easily with others. Because you are relaxed and at ease, you can recognize possibilities as they present themselves, sometimes even before others can see them. Because you are in tune with your own nature, you understand that existence is providing you with exactly what you need. Enjoy the flight! And celebrate all the varied wonders of the landscape spread before you.

POSSIBILITIES

✦   ✦   ✦

MIND CAN ACCEPT any boundary anywhere. But the reality is that, by its very nature, existence cannot have any boundary, because what will be beyond the boundary? – again another sky. That's why I am saying skies upon skies are available for your flight.

Don't be content easily. Those who remain content easily remain small: small are their joys, small are their ecstasies, small are their silences, small is their being.

But there is no need!

This smallness is your own imposition upon your freedom, upon your unlimited possibilities, upon your unlimited potential.[40]

An 'experience' is something that can be filed away in a notebook, or captured on film and pasted into an album. 'Experiencing' is the feeling of wonder itself, the thrill of communion, the gentle touch of our connectedness with all that surrounds us. ✦ The woman in this card is not just touching this tree, she is in communion with it, she has almost become one with it. It is an old tree, and has seen many hard times. Her touch is gentle, reverent, and the white on the inside of her cape reflects the purity of her heart. She is humble, simple — and that is the right way to approach nature. ✦ Nature doesn't bang any drums when it bursts forth into flower, nor play any dirges when the trees let go of their leaves in the fall. But when we approach her in the right spirit, she has many secrets to share. If you haven't heard nature whispering to you lately, now is a good time to give her the opportunity.

EXPERIENCING

✦ ✦ ✦

YOU JUST LOOK AROUND, look into the eyes of a child, or into the eyes of your beloved, your mother, your friend – or just feel a tree.

Have you ever hugged a tree? Hug a tree, and one day you will come to know that it is not only that you have hugged the tree but that the tree also responds, the tree also hugs you. Then for the first time you will be able to know that the tree is not just the form, it is not just a certain species the botanists talk about, it is an unknown God – so green in your courtyard, so full of flowers in your courtyard, so close to you, beckoning you, calling you again and again.[41]

E ach figure in this mandala holds the right hand up, in an attitude of receiving, and the left hand down, in an attitude of giving. The whole circle creates a tremendous energy field that takes on the shape of the double dorje, the Tibetan symbol for the thunderbolt. The mandala has a quality like that of the energy field that forms around a buddha, where all the individuals taking part in the circle make a unique contribution to create a unified and vital whole. It is like a flower, whose wholeness is even more beautiful than the sum of its parts, at the same time enhancing the beauty of each individual petal.

✦ You have an opportunity to participate with others now to make your contribution to creating something greater and more beautiful than each of you could manage alone. Your participation will not only nourish you, but will also contribute something precious to the whole.

PARTICIPATION

✦   ✦   ✦

Have you ever seen night going? Very few people even become aware of things which are happening every day. Have you ever seen the evening coming? The midnight and its song? The sunrise and its beauty? We are behaving almost like blind people. In such a beautiful world we are living in small ponds of our own misery. It is familiar, so even if somebody wants to pull you out, you struggle. You don't want to be pulled out of your misery, of your suffering. Otherwise there is so much joy all around, you have just to be aware of it and to become a participant, not a spectator.

Philosophy is speculation, Zen is participation. Participate in the night leaving, participate in the evening coming, participate in the stars and participate in the clouds; make participation your lifestyle and the whole existence becomes such a joy, such an ecstasy. You could not have dreamed of a better universe.[42]

These three women are high in the air, playful and free, yet alert and interdependent. In a trapeze act, nobody can afford to be a little bit 'absent' even for a split second. And it is this quality of total attentiveness to the moment at hand that is represented here. ✦ We may feel there are too many things to do at once, but get bogged down in trying to do a bit here, a bit there, instead of taking one task at a time and getting on with it. Or perhaps we think our task is 'boring' because we've forgotten that it's not what you do but how you do it that matters. Developing the knack of being total in responding to whatever comes, as it comes, is one of the greatest gifts you can give yourself. Taking one step through life at a time, giving each step your complete attention and energy, can bring a wondrous new vitality and creativity to all that you do.

TOTALITY

✦   ✦   ✦

EVERY MOMENT there is a possibility to be total. What-soever you are doing, be absorbed in it so utterly that the mind thinks nothing, is just there, is just a presence. And more and more totality will be coming. And the taste of totality will make you more and more capable of being total.

And try to see when you are not total. Those are the moments which have to be dropped slowly, slowly. When you are not total, whenever you are in the head – thinking, brooding, calculating, cunning, clever – you are not total. Slowly, slowly slip out of those moments. It is just an old habit. Habits die hard. But they die certainly – if one persists, they die.[43]

This character is obviously 'on top of the world' right now, and the whole world is celebrating his success with a tickertape parade! ✦ Because of your willingness to accept the recent challenges of life, you are now — or you soon will be — enjoying a wonderful ride on the tiger of success. Welcome it, enjoy it, and share your joy with others — and remember that all bright parades have a beginning and an end. If you keep this in mind, and squeeze every drop of juice out of the happiness you are experiencing now, you will be able to take the future as it comes without regrets. But don't be tempted to try to hold on to this abundant moment, or coat it in plastic so that it lasts forever. ✦ The greatest wisdom to keep in mind with all the phenomena in the parade of your life, whether they be valleys or peaks, is that 'this too will pass'. Celebrate, yes, and keep on riding the tiger.

SUCCESS

✦   ✦   ✦

certain.[45]

WATCH THE WAVES in the ocean. The higher the wave goes, the deeper is the wake that follows it. One moment you are the wave, another moment you are the hollow wake that follows. Enjoy both – don't get addicted to one. Don't say: I would always like to be on the peak. It is not possible. Simply see the fact: it is not possible. It has never happened and it will never happen. It is simply impossible – not in the nature of things. Then what to do?

Enjoy the peak while it lasts and then enjoy the valley when it comes. What is wrong with the valley? What is wrong with being low? It is a relaxation. A peak is an excitement, and nobody can exist continuously in an excitement.[44]

How many people do you know who, just when they were completely overloaded, with too many projects, too many 'balls in the air', have suddenly come down with the flu, or taken a fall and ended up on crutches? That's just the sort of 'bad timing' the little monkey with the pin in his hand is about to impose on the 'one-man-band' pictured here! ✦ The quality of stress represented by this card visits all of us at times, but perfectionists are particularly vulnerable to it. We create it ourselves, with the idea that without us nothing will happen — especially in the way we want it to! Well, what makes you think you're so special? Do you think the sun won't rise in the morning unless you personally set the alarm? Go for a walk, buy some flowers, and fix yourself a spaghetti dinner — anything 'unimportant' will do. Just put yourself out of that monkey's reach!

STRESS

✦   ✦   ✦

ALL PRIVATE GOALS ARE NEUROTIC. The essential man comes to know, to feel, "I am not separate from the whole, and there is no need to seek and search for any destiny on my own. Things are happening, the world is moving – call it God…he is doing things. They are happening of their own accord. There is no need for me to make any struggle, any effort; there is no need

for me to fight for anything. I can relax and be."

The essential man is not a doer. The accidental man is a doer. The accidental man is, of course, then in anxiety, tension, stress, anguish, continuously sitting on a volcano. It can erupt any moment, because he lives in a world of uncertainty and believes as if it is certain. This creates tension in his be-ing: he knows deep down that nothing is

T he tiny figure moving on the path through this beautiful landscape is not concerned about the goal. He or she knows that the journey is the goal, the pilgrimage itself is the sacred place. Each step on the path is important in itself. ✦ When this card appears in a reading, it indicates a time of movement and change. It may be a physical movement from one place to the next, or an inner movement from one way of being to another. But whatever the case, this card promises that the going will be easy and will bring a sense of adventure and growth; there is no need to struggle or plan too much. The Traveling card also reminds us to accept and embrace the new, just as when we travel to another country with a different culture and environment than the one we are accustomed to. This attitude of openness and acceptance invites new friends and experiences into our lives.

TRAVELING

✦   ✦   ✦

LIFE IS A CONTINUITY always and always. There is no final destination it is going towards. Just the pilgrimage, just the journey in itself is life, not reaching to some point, no goal – just dancing and being in pilgrimage, moving joyously, without bothering about any destination. What will you do by getting to a destination? Nobody has asked this, because everybody is trying to have some destination in life. But the implications…

If you really reach the destination of life, then what? Then you will look very embarrassed. Nowhere to go…you have reached to the final destination – and in the journey you have lost everything. You had to lose everything. So standing naked at the final destination, you will look all around like an idiot: what was the point? You were hurrying so hard, and you were worrying so hard, and this is the outcome.[46]

This is the portrait of one whose whole life energy has been depleted in his efforts to keep fueling the enormous and ridiculous machine of self-importance and productivity. He has been so busy 'keeping it all together' and 'making sure everything runs smoothly', that he has forgotten to really rest. No doubt he can't allow himself to be playful. To abandon his duty for a trip to the beach could mean the whole structure might come tumbling down. ✦ The message of this card is not just about being a workaholic, though. It is about all the ways in which we set up safe but unnatural routines for ourselves and, by doing so, keep the chaotic and spontaneous away from our doors. Life isn't a business to be managed, it's a mystery to be lived. It's time to tear up the time-card, break out of the factory, and take a little trip into the uncharted. Your work can flow more smoothly from a relaxed state of mind.

Exhaustion

✦ ✦ ✦

A MAN WHO LIVES THROUGH conscience becomes hard. A man who lives through consciousness remains soft. Why? — because a man who has some ideas about how to live, naturally becomes hard. He has continuously to carry his character around himself. That character is like an armor; his protection, his security; his whole life is invested in that character. And he always reacts to situations through the character, not directly. If you ask him a question, his answer is ready-made.

That is the sign of a hard person – he is dull, stupid, mechanical. He may be a good computer, but he is not a man. You do something and he reacts in a well-established way. His reaction is predictable; he is a robot.

The real man acts spontaneously. If you ask him a question, your question gets a response, not a reaction. He opens his heart to your question, exposes himself to your question, responds to it....[47]

The figure on this card is quite literally 'all tied up in knots'. His light still shines within, but he has repressed his own vitality trying to meet so many demands and expectations. He has given up all his own power and vision in return for being accepted by the very same forces that have imprisoned him. The danger of suppressing one's natural energy in this way is apparent in the cracks of a volcanic eruption about to take place around the edges of the image.

✦ The real message of the card is to find a healing outlet for this potential explosion. It is essential to find a way to release whatever tensions and stresses might be building up inside you right now. Beat on a pillow, jump up and down, go out into the wilderness and scream at the empty sky — anything to shake up your energy and allow it to circulate freely. Don't wait for a catastrophe to happen.

SUPPRESSION

✦ ✦ ✦

IN SANSKRIT the name is *alaya vigyan*, the house where you go on throwing into the basement things that you want to do but you cannot, because of social conditions, culture, civilization. But they go on collecting there, and they affect your actions, your life, very indirectly. Directly, they cannot face you – you have forced them into darkness, but from the dark side they go on influencing your behavior. They are dangerous, it is dangerous to keep all those inhibitions inside you.

It is possible that these are the things that come to a climax when a person goes insane. Insanity is nothing but all these suppressions coming to a point where you cannot control them anymore. But madness is acceptable, while meditation is not – and meditation is the only way to make you absolutely sane.[48]

When we speak of being 'grounded' or 'centered' it is this Source we are talking about. When we begin a creative project, it is this Source that we tune in to. ✦ This card reminds us that there is a vast reservoir of energy available to us. And that we tap into it not by thinking and planning but by getting grounded, centered, and silent enough to be in contact with the Source. It is within each of us, like a personal, individual sun giving us life and nourishment. Pure energy, pulsating, available, it is ready to give us anything we need to accomplish something, and ready to welcome us back home when we want to rest. ✦ So whether you are beginning something new and need inspiration right now, or you've just finished something and want to rest, go to the Source. It's always waiting for you, and you don't even have to step out of your house to find it.

THE SOURCE

✦　　✦　　✦

ZEN ASKS YOU TO COME OUT of the head and go to the basic source.... It is not that Zen is not aware of the uses of energy in the head, but if all the energy is used in the head, you will never become aware of your eternity....

You will never know as an experience what it is to be one with the whole.

When the energy is just at the center, pulsating, when it is not moving anywhere, neither in the head nor in the heart, but it is at the very source from where the heart takes it, the head takes it, pulsating at the very source – that is the very meaning of Zazen.

Zazen means just sitting at the very source, not moving anywhere, a tremendous force arises, a transformation of energy into light and love, into greater life, into compassion, into creativity. It can take many forms. But first you have to learn how to be at the source. Then the source will decide where your potential is. You can relax at the source, and it will take you to your very potential.[49]

The branches of these two flowering trees are intertwined, and their fallen petals blend together on the ground in their beautiful colors. It is as if heaven and earth are bridged by love. But they stand individually, each rooted in the soil in their own connection with the earth. In this way they represent the essence of true friends, mature, easy with each other, natural. There is no urgency about their connection, no neediness, no desire to change the other into something else.

✦ This card indicates a readiness to enter this quality of friendliness. In the passage, you may notice that you are no longer interested in all kinds of dramas and romances that other people are engaged in. It is not a loss. It is the birth of a higher, more loving quality born of the fullness of experience. It is the birth of a love that is truly unconditional, without expectations or demands.

FRIENDLINESS

✦ ✦ ✦

FIRST MEDITATE, be blissful, then much love will happen of its own accord. Then being with others is beautiful and being alone is also beautiful. Then it is simple, too. You don't depend on others and you don't make others dependent on you. Then it is always a friendship, a friendliness. It never becomes a relationship, it is always a relatedness.

You relate, but you don't create a marriage. Marriage is out of fear, relatedness is out of love.

You relate; as long as things are moving beautifully, you share. And if you see that the moment has come to depart because your paths separate at this crossroad, you say goodbye with great gratitude for all that the other has been to you, for all the joys and all the pleasures and all the beautiful moments that you have shared with the other. With no misery, with no pain, you simply separate.[50]

These three women dancing in the wind and the rain remind us that celebration never need depend on outside circumstances. We need not wait for a special holiday or a formal occasion, nor a sunny and cloudless day. True celebration arises from a joy that is first experienced deep within, and spills over into an overflow of song and dance and laughter, and yes, even tears of gratitude. ✦ When you choose this card, it indicates that you are becoming more and more available and open to the many opportunities that are to celebrate in life, and to spread this by contagion to others. Don't bother about scheduling a party on your calendar. Let your hair down, take your shoes off, and start splashing in the puddles right now. The party is happening all around you every moment!

CELEBRATION

✦   ✦   ✦

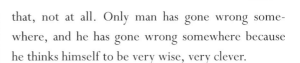

LIFE IS A MOMENT TO CELEBRATE, to enjoy. Make it fun, a celebration, and then you will enter the temple. The temple is not for the long-faced, it has never been for them. Look at life – do you see sadness anywhere? Have you ever seen a tree depressed? Have you seen a bird anxiety-ridden? Have you seen an animal neurotic? No, life is not like that, not at all. Only man has gone wrong somewhere, and he has gone wrong somewhere because he thinks himself to be very wise, very clever.

Your cleverness is your disease. Don't be too wise. Always remember to stop; don't go to the extreme. A little foolishness and a little wisdom is good, and the right combination makes you a buddha...[51]

The woman in this image has a faint smile on her face. In fact she is just watching the antics of the mind — not judging, not trying to stop them, not identified, just watching as if they were traffic on the road, or ripples on the surface of a pond. And the antics of the mind are slightly amusing, as it jumps up and down and twists this way and that, trying to get your attention and seduce you into the game. ✦ To develop the knack of taking a distance from the mind is one of the greatest blessings. It is what meditation is all about really — not chanting a mantra, or repeating an affirmation, but just watching, as if the mind belongs to somebody else. You are ready to take this distance now, and to watch the show without getting caught up in the drama. Indulge yourself in the simple freedom of Turning In whenever you can, and the knack of meditation will grow and deepen in you.

TURNING IN

✦   ✦   ✦

TURNING INWARDS is not a turning at all. Going inwards is not a going at all. Turning inwards simply means that you have been running after this desire and that, and you have been running and running and you have been coming again and again to frustration. That each desire brings misery, that there is no fulfillment through desire. That you never reach anywhere, that contentment is impossible. Seeing this truth, that running after desires takes you nowhere, you stop. Not that you make any effort to stop. If you make any effort to stop it is again running, in a subtle way. You are still desiring – maybe now it is desirelessness that you desire.

If you are making an effort to go in, you are still going out. Any effort can only take you out, outwards.

All journeys are outward journeys, there is no inward journey. How can you journey inwards? You are already there, there is no point in going. When going stops, journeying disappears; when desiring is no more clouding your mind, you are in. This is called turning in. But it is not a turning at all, it is simply not going out.[52]

The figure pictured in this card is so preoccupied with clutching her box of memories that she has turned her back on the sparkling champagne glass of blessings available here and now. Her nostalgia for the past really makes her a 'blockhead', and a beggar besides, as we can see from her patched and ragged clothes. She needn't be a beggar, of course — but she is not available to taste the pleasures that offer themselves in the present. ✦ It's time to face up to the fact that the past is gone, and any effort to repeat it is a sure way to stay stuck in old blueprints that you would have already outgrown if you hadn't been so busy clinging to what you have already been through. Take a deep breath, put the box down, tie it up in a pretty ribbon if you must, and bid it a fond and reverent farewell. Life is passing you by, and you're in danger of becoming an old fossil before your time!

CLINGING TO THE PAST

✦ ✦ ✦

THESE TENSES – past, present and future – are not the tenses of time; they are tenses of the mind. That which is no longer before the mind becomes the past. That which is before the mind is the present. And that which is going to be before the mind is the future.

Past is that which is no longer before you.

Future is that which is not yet before you.

And present is that which is before you and is slipping out of your sight. Soon it will be past....

If you don't cling to the past...because clinging to the past is absolute stupidity. It is no longer there, so you are crying for spilled milk. What is gone is gone! And don't cling to the present because that is also going and soon it will be past. Don't cling to the future – hopes, imaginations, plans for tomorrow – because tomorrow will become today, will become yesterday. Everything is going to become yesterday. Everything is going to go out of your hands.

Clinging will simply create misery.

You will have to let go.[53]

*S*ome enchanted evening you're going to meet your soulmate, the perfect person who will meet all your needs and fulfill all your dreams. Right? Wrong! This fantasy that songwriters and poets are so fond of perpetuating has its roots in memories of the womb, where we were so secure and 'at one' with our mothers; it's no wonder we have hankered to return to that place all our lives. But, to put it quite brutally, it is a childish dream. And it's amazing we hang on to it so stubbornly in the face of reality. ✦ Nobody, whether it's your current mate or some dreamed-of partner in the future, has any obligation to deliver your happiness on a platter — nor could they even if they wanted to. Real love comes not from trying to solve our neediness by depending on another, but by developing our own inner richness and maturity. Then we have so much love to give that we naturally draw lovers towards us.

THE DREAM

✦   ✦   ✦

THIS HAS BEEN SAID again and again, down through the ages. All the religious people have been saying this: "We come alone into this world, we go alone." All togetherness is illusory. The very idea of togetherness arises because we are alone, and the aloneness hurts. We want to drown our aloneness in relationship....

That's why we become so much involved in love. Try to see the point. Ordinarily you think you have fallen in love with a woman or with a man because she is beautiful, he is beautiful. That is not the truth. The truth is just the opposite: you have fallen in love because you cannot be alone. You were going to fall. You were going to avoid yourself somehow or other. And there are people who don't fall in love with women or men – then they fall in love with money. They start moving into money or into a power trip, they become politicians. That too is avoiding your aloneness. If you watch man, if you watch yourself deeply, you will be surprised – all your activities can be reduced to one single source. The source is that you are afraid of your aloneness. Everything else is just an excuse. The real cause is that you find yourself very alone.[54]

The man and woman in this card are facing each other, yet they are not able to see each other clearly. Each is projecting an image they have constructed in their minds, covering the real face of the person they are looking at. ✦ All of us can get caught up in projecting movies of our own making onto the situations and people surrounding us. It happens when we are not fully aware of our own expectations, desires and judgments; instead of taking responsibility for them and owning them, we try to attribute them to others. A projection can be devilish or divine, disturbing or comforting, but it is a projection nonetheless — a cloud that prevents us from seeing reality as it is. The only way out is to recognize the game. When you find a judgment arising about another, turn it around: Does what you see in others really belong to you? Is your vision clear, or clouded by what you want to see?

PROJECTIONS

✦   ✦   ✦

IN A CINEMA HALL, you look at the screen, you never look at the back – the projector is at the back. The film is not there really on the screen; it is just a projection of shadow and light. The film exists just at the back, but you never look at that. And the projector is there.

Your mind is at the back of the whole thing, and the mind is the projector. But you always look at the other, because the other is the screen.

When you are in love the person seems beautiful, no comparison. When you hate, the same person seems the ugliest, and you never become aware of how the same person can be the ugliest and the same person can be the most beautiful....

So the only way to reach to truth is to learn how to be immediate in your vision, how to drop the help of the mind. This agency of the mind is the problem, because mind can create only dreams.... Through your excitement the dream starts looking like reality. If you are too excited then you are intoxicated, then you are not in your senses. Then whatsoever you see is just your projection. And there are as many worlds as there are minds, because every mind lives in his own world.[55]

I n this image of lotus leaves in the early morning, we can see in the rippling of the water that one drop has just fallen. It is a precious moment, and one that is full of poignancy. In surrendering to gravity and slipping off the leaf, the drop loses its previous identity and joins the vastness of the water below. We can imagine that it must have trembled before it fell, just on the edge between the known and the unknowable. ✦ To choose this card is a recognition that something is finished, something is completing. Whatever it is — a job, a relationship, a home you have loved, anything that might have helped you to define who you are — it is time to let go of it, allowing any sadness but not trying to hold on. Something greater is awaiting you, new dimensions are there to be discovered. You are past the point of no return now, and gravity is doing its work. Go with it — it represents liberation.

LETTING GO

✦ ✦ ✦

IN EXISTENCE there is nobody who is superior and nobody who is inferior. The blade of grass and the great star are absolutely equal....
But man wants to be higher than others, he wants to conquer nature, hence he has to fight continuously. All complexity arises out of this fight. The innocent person is one who has renounced fighting; who is no longer interested in being higher, who is no longer interested in performing, in proving that he is someone special; who has become like a roseflower or like a dewdrop on the lotus leaf; who has become part of this infinity; who has melted, merged and become one with the ocean and is just a wave; who has no idea of the 'I'. The disappearance of the 'I' is innocence.[56]

This gentleman clearly thinks he's got it made. He sits in his big overstuffed chair, wearing his sunglasses, shaded by his umbrella, with his pink slippers and his piña colada in his hand. He doesn't have the energy to get up and do anything because he thinks he's done it already. He hasn't yet turned to see the mirror cracking around him on his right, a sure sign that the place he thinks he's finally arrived at is about to shatter and dissolve before his very eyes. ✦ The message this card brings is that this poolside resort is not your final destination. The journey isn't over yet, as that white bird flying into the vastness of the sky is trying to show. Your complacency might have arisen from a real sense of achievement, but now it's time to move on. No matter how fuzzy the slippers, how tasty the piña colada, there are skies upon skies still waiting to be explored.

LAZINESS

✦   ✦   ✦

WHEN YOU ARE LAZY, it is a negative taste: you simply feel that you have no energy, you simply feel dull; you simply feel sleepy, you simply feel dead. When you are in a state of non-doing then you are full of energy – it is a very positive taste. You have full energy, overflowing. You are radiant, bubbling, vibrating, You are not sleepy, you are perfectly aware. You are not dead – you are tremendously alive....

There is a possibility the mind can deceive you: it can rationalize laziness as non-doing. It can say, "I have become a Zen master," or, "I believe in Tao" – but you are not deceiving anybody else. You will be deceiving only yourself. So be alert.[57]

The experience of resting in the heart in meditation is not something that can be grasped or forced. It comes naturally, as we grow more and more in tune with the rhythms of our own inner silences. The figure on this card reflects the sweetness and delicacy of this experience. The dolphins that emerge from the heart and make an arc towards the third eye reflect the playfulness and intelligence that comes when we are able to connect with the heart and move into the world from there. ✦ Let yourself be softer and more receptive now, because an inexpressible joy is waiting for you just around the corner. Nobody else can point it out to you, and when you find it you won't be able to find the words to express it to others. But it's there, deep within your heart, ripe and ready to be discovered.

HARMONY

✦   ✦   ✦

L ISTEN TO YOUR HEART, move according to your heart, whatsoever the stake:

A condition of complete simplicity costing not less than everything....

To be simple is arduous, because to be simple costs everything that you have. You have to lose all to be simple.

That's why people have chosen to be complex and they have forgotten how to be simple.

But only a simple heart throbs with God, hand in hand. Only a simple heart sings with God in deep harmony. To reach to that point you will have to find your heart, your own throb, your own beat.[58]

The figure in this card is completely relaxed and at ease in the water, letting it take him where it will. He has mastered the art of being passive and receptive without being dull or sleepy. He is just available to the currents of life, with never a thought of saying "I don't like that," or "I prefer to go the other way." ◆ Every moment in life we have a choice whether to enter life's waters and float, or to try to swim upstream. When this card appears in a reading it is an indication that you are able to float now, trusting that life will support you in your relaxation and take you exactly where it wants you to go. Allow this feeling of trust and relaxation to grow more and more; everything is happening exactly as it should.

GOING WITH THE FLOW

✦ ✦ ✦

WHEN I SAY 'become water' I mean become a flow; don't remain stagnant. Move, and move like water. Lao Tzu says: The way of the Tao is a watercourse way. It moves like water. What is the movement of water? or of a river? The movement has a few beautiful things about it. One, it always moves towards the depth, it always searches for the lowest ground. It is non-ambitious; it never hankers to be the first, it wants to be the last.

Remember, Jesus says: Those who are the last here will be the first in my kingdom of God. He is talking about the watercourse way of Tao – not mentioning it, but talking about it. Be the last, be non-ambitious. Ambition means going uphill. Water goes down, it searches for the lowest ground, it wants to be a nonentity. It does not want to declare itself unique, exceptional, extraordinary. It has no ego idea.[59]

The person on this card brings a new twist to the old idea of 'getting stuck between a rock and a hard place'! But we are in precisely this sort of situation when we get stuck in the indecisive and dualistic aspect of the mind. Should I let my arms go and fall head-first, or let my legs go and fall feet-first? Should I go here or there? Should I say yes or no? And whatever decision we make, we will always wonder if we should have decided the other way. ✦ The only way out of this dilemma is, unfortunately, to let go of both at once. You can't work your way out of this one by solving it, making lists of pros and cons, or in any way working it out with your mind. Better to follow your heart, if you can find it. If you can't find it, just jump — your heart will start beating so fast there will be no mistake about where it is!

SCHIZOPHRENIA

✦   ✦   ✦

MAN IS SPLIT. Schizophrenia is a normal condition of man – at least now. It may not have been so in the primitive world, but centuries of conditioning, civilization, culture and religion have made man a crowd – divided, split, contradictory.... But because this split is against his nature, deep down somewhere hidden the unity still survives. Because the soul of man is one, all the conditionings at the most destroy the periphery of the man. But the center remains untouched – that's how man continues to live. But his life has become a hell.

The whole effort of Zen is how to drop this schizophrenia, how to drop this split personality, how to drop the divided mind of man, how to become undivided, integrated, centered, crystallized.

The way you are, you cannot say that you are. You don't have a being. You are a marketplace – many voices. If you want to say 'yes', immediately the 'no' is there. You cannot even utter a simple word 'yes' with totality.... In this way happiness is not possible; unhappiness is a natural consequence of a split personality.[60]

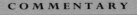

In our society, men in particular have been taught not to cry, to put a brave face on things when they get hurt and not show that they are in pain. But women can fall into this trap too, and all of us at one time or another might feel that the only way to survive is to close off our feelings and emotions so we can't be hurt again. If our pain is particularly deep, we might even try to hide it from ourselves. This can make us frozen, rigid, because deep down we know that one small break in the ice will free the hurt to start circulating through us again. ◆ The rainbow-colored tears on this person's face hold the key to breaking out of this 'ice-olation'. The tears, and only the tears, have the power to melt the ice. It's okay to cry, and there is no reason to feel ashamed of your tears. Crying helps us to let go of pain, allows us to be gentle with ourselves, and finally helps us to heal.

ICE-OLATION

✦   ✦   ✦

W̲E ARE MISERABLE because we are too much in the self. What does it mean when I say we are too much in the self? And what exactly happens when we are too much in the self? Either you can be in existence or you can be in the self – both are not possible together. To be in the self means to be apart, to be separate. To be in the self means to become an island. To be in the self means to draw a boundary line around you. To be in the self means to make a distinction between 'this I am' and 'that I am not'. The definition, the boundary, between 'I' and 'not I' is what the self is – the self isolates. And it makes you frozen – you are no longer flowing. If you are flowing the self cannot exist. Hence people have become almost like ice-cubes. They don't have any warmth, they don't have any love – love is warmth and they are afraid of love. If warmth comes to them they will start melting and the boundaries will disappear. In love the boundaries disappear; in joy also the boundaries disappear, because joy is not cold.[61]

The woman in this picture is living in a gray landscape, full of unreal, cut-out clouds. Through the window frame she can see colors and light and aliveness, and although she would like to move through the frame — as we can see by the rainbow colors appearing in her garment — she can't quite manage to do it. There is still too much 'what-if?' activity in her mind. ✦ Tomorrow never comes, they say, but no matter how often it is said, it seems that most of us tend to forget the truth of it. In fact, the one and only result of postponing things is a dull and depressing feeling of incompletion and 'stuck-ness' today. The relief and expansiveness you will feel once you put aside all the dithering thoughts that are preventing you from acting now will make you wonder why you ever waited so long.

POSTPONEMENT

✦   ✦   ✦

POSTPONEMENT IS SIMPLY STUPID. Tomorrow you will also have to decide, so why not today? And do you think that tomorrow you will be wiser than today? Do you think that tomorrow you will be livelier than today? Do you think that tomorrow you will be younger than today, fresher than today?

Tomorrow you will be older, your courage will be less; tomorrow you will be more experienced, your cunningness will be more; tomorrow death will come closer – you will start wavering and being more afraid. Never postpone for the tomorrow. And

who knows? Tomorrow may come or may not come. If you have to decide you have to decide right now.

Dr. Vogel, the dentist, finished his examination on a pretty young patient. "Miss Baseman," he said, "I'm afraid I'm going to have to pull out your wisdom teeth!"

"Oh, my!" exclaimed the girl. "I'd rather have a baby!"

"Well," said Dr. Vogel, "could you make up your mind so that I can adjust the chair?"

Make up your mind. Don't go on postponing infinitely.[62]

W*ho ever told you that the bamboo is more beautiful than the oak, or the oak more valuable than the bamboo? Do you think the oak wishes it had a hollow trunk like this bamboo? Does the bamboo feel jealous of the oak because it is bigger and its leaves change color in the fall? The very idea of the two trees comparing themselves to each other seems ridiculous, but we humans seem to find this habit very hard to break.* ✦ *Let's face it, there is always going to be somebody who is more beautiful, more talented, stronger, more intelligent, or apparently happier than you are. And conversely, there will always be those who are* less *than you in all these ways. The way to find out who you are is not by comparing yourself with others, but by looking to see whether you are fulfilling your own potential in the best way you know how.*

COMPARISON

✦   ✦   ✦

COMPARISON BRINGS inferiority, superiority. When you don't compare, all inferiority, all superiority, disappear. Then you are, you are simply there. A small bush or a big high tree – it doesn't matter; you are yourself. You are needed. A grass leaf is needed as much as the biggest star. Without the grass leaf God will be less than he is. This sound of the cuckoo is needed as much as any Buddha; the world will be less, will be less rich if this cuckoo disappears.

Just look around. All is needed, and everything fits together. It is an organic unity: nobody is higher and nobody is lower, nobody superior, nobody inferior. Everybody is incomparably unique.[63]

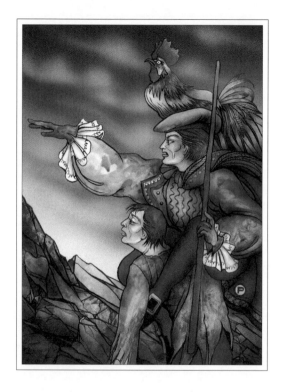

When we carry a load of shoulds and shouldn'ts imposed on us by others we become like this ragged, struggling figure trying to make his way uphill. "Go faster, try harder, reach the top!" shouts the foolish tyrant he carries on his shoulder, while the tyrant himself is crowned with an imperious rooster. ◆ If life these days feels like just a struggle from the cradle to the grave, it could be time to shrug your shoulders and see what it feels like to walk without these characters on your back. You have your own mountains to conquer, your own dreams to fulfill, but you will never have the energy to pursue them until you release yourself from all the expectations you've gathered from others but now think are your own. Chances are they exist only in your own mind, but that doesn't mean they can't weigh you down. It's time to lighten up, and send them on their way.

THE BURDEN

✦ ✦ ✦

A MAN'S TRUE LIFE is the way in which he puts off the lie imposed by others on him. Stripped, naked, natural, he is what he is. This is a matter of being, and not of becoming. The lie cannot become the truth, the personality cannot become your soul. There is no way to make the nonessential the essential. The nonessential remains nonessential and the essential remains essential, they are not convertible. And striving towards truth is nothing but creating more confusion. The truth has not to be achieved. It cannot be achieved, it is already the case. Only the lie has to be dropped.

All aims and ends and ideals and goals and ideologies, religions and systems of improvement and betterment, are lies. Beware of them. Recognize the fact that, as you are, you are a lie. Manipulated, cultivated by others. Striving after truth is a distraction and a postponement. It is the lie's way to hide. See the lie, look deep into the lie of your personality. Because to see the lie is to cease to lie. No longer to lie is to seek no more for any truth – there is no need. The moment the lie disappears, truth is there in all its beauty and radiance. In the seeing of the lie it disappears, and what is left is the truth.[64]

*D*o you recognize this man? All but the most innocent and sincere of us have a politician lurking somewhere in our minds. In fact, the mind is political. Its very nature is to plan and scheme and try to manipulate situations and people so that it can get what it wants. Here, the mind is represented by the snake, covered with clouds and 'speaking with a forked tongue'. But the important thing to realize about this card is that both faces are false. The sweet, innocent, 'trust me' face is a mask, and the evil, toxic, 'I'll have my way with you' face is a mask, too. Politicians don't have real faces. The whole game is a lie.

✦ Take a good look at yourself to see if you have been playing this game. What you see might be painful, but not as painful as continuing to play. It doesn't serve anybody's interest in the end, least of all yours. Whatever you might achieve in this way will just turn to dust in your hands.

POLITICS

✦   ✦   ✦

ANYBODY WHO can be a good pretender, a hypocrite, will become your leader politically, will become your priest religiously. All that he needs is hypocrisy, all that he needs is cunningness, all that he needs is a façade to hide behind. Your politicians live double lives, your priests live double lives – one from the front door, the other from the back door. And the back-door life is their real life. Those front-door smiles are just false, those faces looking so innocent are just cultivated.

If you want to see the reality of the politician you will have to see him from his back door. There he is in his nudity, as he is, and so is the priest. These two kinds of cunning people have dominated humanity. And they found out very early on that if you want to dominate humanity, make it weak, make it feel guilty, make it feel unworthy. Destroy its dignity, take all glory away from it, humiliate it. And they have found such subtle ways of humiliation that they don't come in the picture at all; they leave it to you to humiliate yourself, to destroy yourself. They have taught you a kind of slow suicide.[65]

Guilt is one of the most destructive emotions in which we can get caught. If we have wronged another, or gone against our own truth, then of course we will feel bad. But to let ourselves be overwhelmed with guilt is to invite a migraine. We end up surrounded by nagging clouds of self-doubt and feelings of worthlessness to the point where we cannot see any of the beauty and joy that life is trying to offer us. ✦ We all long to be better people — more loving, more aware, more true to ourselves. But when we punish ourselves for our failures by feeling guilty, we can get locked into a cycle of despair and hopelessness that robs us of all clarity about ourselves and the situations we encounter. You are absolutely okay as you are, and it is absolutely natural to go astray from time to time. Just learn from it, move on, and use the lesson not to make the same mistake again.

GUILT

✦ ✦ ✦

THIS MOMENT!...this herenow...is forgotten when you start thinking in terms of achieving something. When the achieving mind arises, you lose contact with the paradise you are in. This is one of the most liberating approaches: it liberates you right now! Forget all about sin and forget all about saintliness; both are stupid. Both together have destroyed all the joys of humanity. The sinner is feeling guilty, hence his joy is lost. How can you enjoy life if you are continuously feeling guilty? if you are continuously going to the church to confess that you have done this wrong and that wrong? And wrong and wrong and wrong...your whole life seems to be made of sins. How can you live joyously? It becomes impossible to delight in life. You become heavy, loaded. Guilt sits on your chest like a rock, it crushes you; it does not allow you to dance. How can you dance? How can guilt dance? How can guilt sing? How can guilt love? How can guilt live? So the one who thinks he is doing something wrong is guilty, burdened, dead before death, has already entered into the grave.[66]

The image is of Ananda, the cousin and disciple of Gautam Buddha. He was at Buddha's side constantly, attending to his every need for forty-two years. When Buddha died, the story is told that Ananda was still at his side, weeping. The other disciples chastised him for his misunderstanding: Buddha had died absolutely fulfilled; he should be rejoicing. But Ananda said, "You misunderstand. I'm weeping not for him but for myself, because for all these years I have been constantly at his side but I have still not attained." Ananda stayed awake for the whole night, meditating deeply and feeling his pain and sorrow. By the morning, it is said, he was enlightened. ✦ Times of great sorrow have the potential to be times of great transformation. But in order for transformation to happen we must go deep, to the very roots of our pain, and experience it as it is, without blame or self-pity.

SORROW

+   +   +

THIS PAIN is not to make you sad, remember. That's where people go on missing.... This pain is just to make you more *alert* – because people become alert only when the arrow goes deep into their heart and wounds them. Otherwise they don't become alert. When life is easy, comfortable, convenient, who cares? Who bothers to become alert? When a friend dies, there is a possibility. When your woman leaves you alone – those dark nights, you are lonely. You have loved that woman so much and you have staked all, and then suddenly one day she is gone. Crying in your loneliness, those are the occasions when, if you use them, you can become aware. The arrow is hurting: it can be used.

The pain is not to make you miserable, the pain is to make you more aware! And when you are aware, misery disappears.[67]

This card depicts the evolution of consciousness as it is described by Friedrich Nietzsche in his book, **Thus Spake** Zarathustra. *He speaks of the three levels of Camel, Lion and Child. The camel is sleepy, dull, self-satisfied. He lives in delusion, thinking he's a mountain peak, but really he is so concerned with others' opinions that he hardly has any energy of his own. Emerging from the camel is the lion. When we realize we've been missing life, we start saying no to the demands of others. We move out of the crowd, alone and proud, roaring our truth. But this is not the end. Finally the child emerges, neither acquiescent nor rebellious, but innocent and spontaneous and true to his own being.* ✦ *Whatever the space you're in right now — sleepy and depressed, or roaring and rebellious — be aware that it will evolve into something new if you allow it. It is a time of growth and change.*

REBIRTH

✦ ✦ ✦

IN ZEN YOU ARE coming from nowhere and you are going to nowhere. You are just now, here, neither coming nor going. Everything passes by you; your consciousness reflects it but it does not get identified.

When a lion roars in front of a mirror, do you think the mirror roars? Or when the lion is gone and a child comes dancing, the mirror completely forgets about the lion and starts dancing with the child – do you think the mirror dances with the child? The mirror does nothing, it simply reflects.

Your consciousness is only a mirror.

Neither do you come, nor do you go.

Things come and go.

You become young, you become old; you are alive, you are dead.

All these states are simply reflections in an eternal pool of consciousness.[68]

M *ost of the cards in this suit of the mind are either cartoon-like or troubled, because the influence of the mind in our lives is generally either ridiculous or oppressive. But this card of Consciousness shows a vast Buddha figure. He is so expansive he has gone even beyond the stars, and above his head is pure emptiness. He represents the consciousness that is available to all who become a master of the mind and can use it as the servant it is meant to be.* ✦ *When you choose this card, it means that there is a crystal clarity available right now, detached, rooted in the deep stillness that lies at the core of your being. There is no desire to understand from the perspective of the mind — the understanding you have now is existential, whole, in harmony with the pulse of life itself. Accept this great gift, and share it.*

CONSCIOUSNESS

✦   ✦   ✦

WE COME FROM the unknown and we go on moving into the unknown. We will come again; we have been here thousands of times, and we will be here thousands of times. Our essential being is immortal but our body, our embodiment, is mortal. Our frame in which we are, our houses, the body, the mind, they are made of material things. They will get tired, they will get old, they will die. But your consciousness, for which Bodhidharma uses the word 'no-mind' – Gautam Buddha has also used the word 'no-mind' – is something beyond body and mind, something beyond everything; that no-mind is eternal. It comes into expression, and goes again into the unknown.

This movement from the unknown to the known, and from the known to the unknown, continues for eternity, unless somebody becomes enlightened. Then that is his last life; then this flower will not come back again. This flower that has become aware of itself need not come back to life because life is nothing but a school in which to learn. He has learned the lesson, he is now beyond delusions. He will move from the known for the first time not into the unknown, but into the unknowable.[69]

As this figure moves across the stones, he steps lightly and non-seriously, and at the same time absolutely balanced and alert. Behind the swirling, ever-changing waters we can see the shapes of buildings; there appears to be a city in the background. The man is in the marketplace but at the same time outside of it, maintaining his balance and able to watch it from above. ✦ This card challenges us to move away from our preoccupations with other spaces and other times, and stay alert to what is happening in the here and now. Life is a great ocean in which you can play if you drop all your judgments, your preferences.and the attachment to the details of your long-term plans. Be available to what comes your way, as it comes. And don't worry if you stumble or fall; just pick yourself up, dust yourself off, have a good laugh, and carry on.

MOMENT TO MOMENT

✦   ✦   ✦

THE PAST IS NO MORE and the future is not yet: both are unnecessarily moving in directions which don't exist. One used to exist, but no longer exists, and one has not even started to exist. The only right person is one who lives moment to moment, whose arrow is directed to the moment, who is always here and now; wherever he is, his whole consciousness, his whole being, is involved in the reality of here and in the reality of now. That's the only right direction. Only such a man can enter into the golden gate.

The present is the golden gate.

Here-now is the golden gate.

…And you can be in the present only if you are not ambitious – no accomplishment, no desire to achieve power, money, prestige, even enlightenment, because all ambition leads you into the future. Only a non-ambitious man can remain in the present.

A man who wants to be in the present has not to think, has just to see and enter the gate. Experience will come, but experience has not to be premeditated.[70]

T he angelic figure with rainbow-colored wings on this card
represents the guide that each of us carries within. Like
the second figure in the background, we may sometimes be a
little reluctant to trust this guide when it comes to us, because
we are so accustomed to taking our cues from the outside rather
than from the inside. ✦ The truth of your own deepest being is
trying to show you where to go right now, and when this card
appears it means you can trust the inner guidance you are being
given. It speaks in whispers, and sometimes we can hesitate, not
knowing if we have understood rightly. But the indications are
clear: in following the inner guide you will feel more whole,
more integrated, as if you are moving outwards from the very
center of your being. If you go with it, this beam of light will
carry you exactly where you need to go.

GUIDANCE

✦ ✦ ✦

YOU HAVE TO LOOK for guidance because you don't know your inner guide is hidden inside you. You have to find the inner guide, and that's what I call your witness. That's what I call your *dharma,* that's what I call your intrinsic buddha. You have to awaken that buddha and your life will shower blessings, benediction. Your life will become so radiant with good, with godliness, more than you can possibly conceive.

It is almost like light. Your room is dark, just bring light in. Even a small candle will do, and the whole darkness disappears. And once you have a candle you know where the door is. You don't have to think about it: "Where is the door?" Only blind people think about where the door is. People who have eyes and the light is there, they don't think. Have you ever thought, "Where is the door?" You simply get up and go out. You never give a single thought to where the door is. You don't start groping for the door or hitting your head against the wall. You simply see, and there is not even a flicker of thought. You simply go out.[71]

This woman has created a fortress around herself, and she is clinging to all the possessions she thinks are her treasures. In fact she has accumulated so much stuff with which to adorn herself — including the feathers and furs of living creatures — that she has made herself ugly in the effort. ✦ This card challenges us to look at what we are clinging to, and what we feel we possess that is so valuable it needs to be protected by a fortress. It needn't be a big bank balance or a box full of jewels — it could be something as simple as sharing our time with a friend, or taking the risk of expressing our love to another. Like a well that is sealed up and becomes stagnant from disuse, our treasures become tarnished and worthless if we refuse to share them. Whatever you're holding on to, remember that you can't take it with you. Loosen your grip and feel the freedom and expansiveness sharing can bring.

THE MISER

✦   ✦   ✦

THE MOMENT YOU BECOME miserly you are closed to the basic phenomenon of life: ex-pansion, sharing.

The moment you start clinging to things, you have missed the target – you have missed. Because things are not the target, you, your innermost being, is the target – not a beautiful house, but a beautiful you; not much money, but a rich you; not many things, but an open being, available to millions of things.[72]

The small child in this card is standing on one side of a gate, looking through it. He is so small, and so convinced that he cannot get through, he cannot see that the chain holding the gate is not locked; all he has to do is open it.

✦ Whenever we feel 'left out', or excluded, it brings up this feeling of being a small, helpless child. It is not surprising, as the feeling is deeply rooted in our earliest childhood experiences. The problem is that, because it is so deeply rooted, it plays over and over again, like a tape, in our lives. You have an opportunity now to stop the tape, to quit tormenting yourself with ideas that you are somehow not 'enough' to be accepted and included. Recognize the roots of these feelings in the past, and let go of the old pain. It will bring you the clarity to see how you can open the gate and enter that which you most long to become.

THE OUTSIDER

✦   ✦   ✦

S O YOU ARE FEELING yourself an outsider. This is good. This is the transitory period. Now you have to be alert not to fill yourself with pain and misery. Now that God is no longer there, who is going to console you? You don't need any consolation. Humanity has come of age. Be a man, be a woman, and stand on your own feet....

The only way to be connected with existence is to go inwards, because there at the center you are still connected. You have been disconnected physically from your mother. That disconnection was absolutely necessary to make you an individual in your own right. But you are not disconnected from the universe. Your connection with the universe is of consciousness. You cannot see it, so you have to go deep down with great awareness, watchfulness, witnessing, and you will find the connection. The buddha is the connection![73]

THE TRANSCENDENTAL GAME OF ZEN ✦ 147

*I*n the courts of ancient Japan, the male attendants were *often selected from the ranks of petty criminals who were castrated. Because of their intimate familiarity with the activities of the court, they were often at the center of the political and social intrigues and excercised a great deal of power behind the scenes. ✦ The two figures on this card remind us of the sleazy and consipritorial situations we can get into when we compromise our own truth. It is one thing to meet another halfway, to understand a point of view different from our own and work towards a harmony of the opposing forces. It is quite another to 'cave in' and betray our own truth. If we look deeply into it, we usually find that we are trying to gain something — whether it is power or the approval of others. If you are tempted, beware: the rewards of this kind of compromise always leave a bitter taste in the mouth.*

COMPROMISE

✦   ✦   ✦

DON'T BE CLEVER, otherwise you will remain the same, you will not change. Half-techniques on the path of love and half-techniques on the path of meditation will create much confusion in you. They will not help....

But to ask for help is against the ego, so you try to compromise. This compromise will be more dangerous, it will confuse you more because, made out of confusion, it will create more confusion.

So try to understand why you hanker for compromise. Sooner or later you will be able to understand that compromise is not going to help. And compromise may be a way of not going in either direction, or it may be just a repression of your confusion. It will assert itself. Never repress anything, be clear-cut about your situation. And if you are confused, remember that you are confused. This will be the first clear-cut thing about you: that you are confused.

You have started on the journey.[74]

T here are times when the only thing to do is to wait. The seed has been planted, the child is growing in the womb, the oyster is coating the grain of sand and making it into a pearl. ✦ This card reminds us that now is a time when all that is required is to be simply alert, patient, waiting. The woman pictured here is in just such an attitude. Contented, with no trace of anxiety, she is simply waiting. Through all the phases of the moon passing overhead she remains patient, so in tune with the rhythms of the moon that she has almost become one with it. She knows it is a time to be passive, letting nature take its course. But she is neither sleepy nor indifferent; she knows it is time to be ready for something momentous. It is a time full of mystery, like the hours just before the dawn. It is a time when the only thing to do is to wait.

PATIENCE

✦   ✦   ✦

WE HAVE FORGOTTEN how to wait; it is almost an abandoned space. And it is our greatest treasure to be able to wait for the right moment. The whole existence waits for the right moment. Even trees know it – when it is time to bring the flowers and when it is time to let go of all the leaves and stand naked against the sky. They are still beautiful in that nakedness, waiting for the new foliage with a great trust that the old has gone, and the new will soon be coming, and the new leaves will start growing. We have forgotten to wait, we want everything in a hurry. It is a great loss to humanity….

In silence and waiting something inside you goes on growing – your authentic being. And one day it jumps and becomes a flame, and your whole personality is shattered; you are a new man. And this new man knows what ceremony is, this new man knows life's eternal juices.[75]

This figure walking in nature shows us that beauty can be found in the simple, ordinary things of life. We so easily take this beautiful world we live in for granted. Cleaning the house, tending the garden, cooking a meal – the most mundane tasks take on a sacred quality when they are performed with your total involvement, with love, and for their own sake, without thought of recognition or reward. ✦ You are facing a time now when this easy, natural and utterly ordinary approach to the situations you encounter will bring far better results than any attempt on your part to be brilliant, clever, or otherwise extra-ordinary. Forget all about making headlines by inventing the latest widget, or dazzling your friends and colleagues with your unique star quality. The special gift you have to offer now is presented best by just taking things easily and simply, one step at a time.

ORDINARINESS

✦ ✦ ✦

SOMETIMES IT HAPPENS that you become one, in some rare moment. Watch the ocean, the tremendous wildness of it – and suddenly you forget your split, your schizophrenia; you relax. Or, moving in the Himalayas, seeing the virgin snow on the Himalayan peaks, suddenly a coolness surrounds you and you need not be false because there is no other human being to be false to. You fall together. Or, listening to beautiful music, you fall together. Whenever, in whatsoever situation, you become one, a peace, a happiness, a bliss, surrounds you, arises in you. You feel fulfilled.

There is no need to wait for these moments – these moments can become your natural life. These extra-ordinary moments can become ordinary moments – that is the whole effort of Zen. You can live an extraordinary life in a very ordinary life: cutting wood, chopping wood, carrying water from the well, you can be tremendously at ease with yourself. Cleaning the floor, cooking food, washing the clothes, you can be perfectly at ease – because the whole question is of you doing your action totally, enjoying, delighting in it.[76]

When the fruit is ripe, it drops from the tree by itself. One moment it hangs by a thread from the branches of the tree, bursting with juice. The next moment it falls — not because it has been forced to fall, or has made the effort to jump, but because the tree has recognized its ripeness and simply let it go. ✦ When this card appears in a reading it indicates that you are ready to share your inner riches, your 'juice'. All you need to do is relax right where you are, and be willing for it to happen. This sharing of yourself, this expression of your creativity, can come in many ways — in your work, your relationships, your everyday life experiences. No special preparation or effort on your part is required. It is simply the right time.

RIPENESS

✦ ✦ ✦

ONLY IF YOUR MEDITATION has brought you a light that shines in every night will even death not be a death to you but a door to the divine. With the light in your heart, death itself is transformed into a door, and you enter into the universal spirit; you become one with the ocean.

And unless you know the oceanic experience, you have lived in vain.

Now is always the time, and the fruit is always ripe. You just need to gather courage to enter into your inner forest. The fruit is always ripe and the time is always the right time. There is no such thing as wrong time.[77]

Humanity is depicted here as a rainbow of beings, dancing around the mandala of the earth with their hands joined together in joy and gratitude for the gift of life. This card represents a time of communication, of sharing the riches that each of us brings to the whole. There is no clinging here, no grasping. It is a circle without fear of feelings of inferiority and superiority. ✦ When we recognize the common source of our humanity, the common origins of our dreams and longings, our hopes and fears, we are able to see that we are all joined together in the great miracle of existence. When we can combine our tremendous inner wealth to create a treasure of love and wisdom that is available to all, we are linked together in the exquisite pattern of eternal creation.

WE ARE THE WORLD

✦   ✦   ✦

WHEN THOUSANDS and thousands of people around the earth are celebrating, singing, dancing, ecstatic, drunk with the divine, there is no possibility of any global suicide. With such festivity and with such laughter, with such sanity and health, with such naturalness and spontaneity, how can there be a war?...

Life has been given to you to create, and to rejoice, and to celebrate. When you cry and weep, when you are miserable, you are alone. When you celebrate, the whole existence participates with you.

Only in celebration do we meet the ultimate, the eternal. Only in celebration do we go beyond the circle of birth and death.[78]

This figure stands alone, silent and yet alert. The inner being is filled with flowers — that carry the quality of springtime and regenerate wherever he goes. This inner flowering and the wholeness that he feels affords the possibility of unlimited movement. He can move in any direction — within and without it makes no difference as his joy and and maturity cannot be diminished by externals. He has come to a time of centeredness and expansiveness — the white glow around the figure is his protection and his light. All of life's experiences have brought him to this time of perfection. ✦ When you draw this card, know well this moment carries a gift — for hard work well done. Your base is solid now and success and good fortune are yours for they are the outcome of what has already been experienced within.

MATURITY

✦ ✦ ✦

The distinction between the grasses and the blossoms is the same as between you *not knowing* that you are a buddha, and the moment you know that you *are* a buddha. In fact, there is no way to be otherwise.

Buddha is completely blossomed, fully opened. His lotuses, his petals, have come to a completion....

Certainly, to be full of spring yourself is far more beautiful than the autumm dews falling on the lotus leaves. That is one of the most beautiful things to watch: when autumm dews fall on the lotus leaves and shine in the morning sun like real pearls. But of course it is a momentary experience. As the sun rises, the autumm dews start evaporating....

This temporary beauty cannot be compared, certainly, with an eternal spring in your being. You look back as far as you can and it has always been there. You look forward as much as you can, and you will be surprised: it is your very being. Wherever you are it will be there, and the flowers will continue to shower on you. This is spiritual spring.[79]

THE DIAMOND

Several sample spreads or layouts are suggested here for you to begin your journey with the Osho Zen Tarot. As with interpreting any of the cards, the positions in which cards are drawn and placed have specific meanings. If you have an intuition that the card is hinting at another meaning, direction, or insight, trust your own intuition and creativity in the reading.

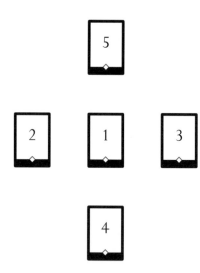

This layout is useful for more clarity on a specific issue.

1. The issue
2. Internal influence that you are unable to see
3. External influence of which you are aware
4. What is needed for resolution
5. Resolution: the understanding

THE FLYING BIRD

This layout is designed in the shape of a bird taking flight. The cards chosen and placed in the left wing symbolize and indicate to us something about our feminine, receptive energies in the moment, while the right wing symbolizes our male, active energies. The first card picked is the initiator of the flight, hence stems from the masculine side. Each succeeding card responds to the previous one and lifts the 'bird' higher, allowing the questioner to move into greater clarity and inner spaciousness.

1 Here & now – the 'lift-off' card
2 The resistance card – 'fear of flying'
3 Response-ability to the fear
4 Inner support (intuition) of responsibility
5 External support (intelligent action responding to the intuition)
6 Relaxation and acceptance
7 Arrival at a new level of awareness

THE KEY

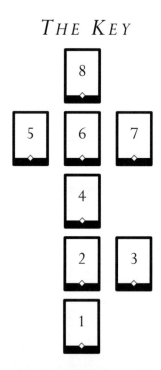

The Key layout can 'open the door' to insight regarding hidden, unconscious aspects of a particular issue. Also, it may be used as a general reading for a here/now insight into your interiority.

1 What is repressed
2 The Yin card, your female (passive) aspect
3 The Yang card, your male (active) aspect
4 The meditation
5 Insight into the body
6 Insight into the heart
7 Insight into the being
8 Consciousness (understanding)

This spread is used to gain insight when relating with another (beloved, friend, relative, etc.). It shows each individual in his/her current life process as well as the composite energies or partnership.

THE MIRROR

12   *Inner spiritual purpose*

1 & 4   The body
2 & 5   The heart
3 & 6   The mind
7 & 10   Melting and merging (intimacy)
8 & 11   The alchemy of togetherness (transformation)
9 & 12   The blessings (benefits and gifts)

You in the here/now

Partner in the here/now

Outer manifestation of the partnership

THE CELTIC CROSS

This traditional layout is used for clarity on a specific issue as well as for general readings. In the Osho Zen Tarot, the positions of the cards have the following meanings:

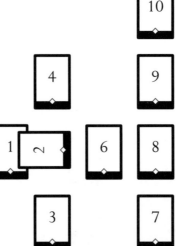

1. The issue
2. Diminishing/enhancing the issue, or clarifying/obscuring the issue
3. The unconscious influences
4. The conscious influences
5. Old patterns, the old way
6. New patterns, moving into the new
7. Self: your feelings and attitudes about the issue
8. What you are attracting from the outside
9. Your desires/denials
10. Outcome/key

RELATING ✦ THE PARADOX

RELATING – 'A QUICKIE'

This spread offers a quick look at your relating with the other, whether 'the other' is your boss, lover, friend, sister, parent, etc.

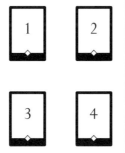

1 You and what you are contributing to the relating here/now
2 The other, the other's input to the relating
3 The composite energies
4 The insight

THE 'SUPER QUICKIE'

A single card – for insight into any situation, or as your meditation for the day.

THE PARADOX

Shuffle the deck of cards for a few minutes. Split the deck into three packs and select one. The top card of the stack you have chosen represents the here/now. The bottom card represents the past-life influences.

Fan the rest of this stack and select one more card. This card represents the insight into the paradox.

Bird Spirit of air, imagination, possibilities, happiness, 'the soul', entering into a higher state of consciousness

Buddha Perfection, pure consciousness, self-realization, ultimate wisdom, compassion, stillness, transcendence of duality

Butterfly Transformation, flightiness, lightness, temporariness, fragility

Camel self-satisfied, unawareness, temperamental foolishness

Chain Conditions, limitations, boundaries

Child Potential, simplicity, innocence, joy, perfection, transmutation

Circle Pure space, spirit, totality, wholeness, femaleness, no beginning no end, self-contained, heaven

Clouds The mind (changing nature of), hiding or covering, light and clarity, hidden blessings, oppression, heaviness, or lightness + non-seriousness, unformed

Colors Violet: Intelligence, balance, equality (red (hot) + blue (cool) = violet

Red: Strength, energy, fire, the sun, passion, sexuality, masculine, active principle
Pink: Love, perfection (red + white = pink; strength + passion and purity = love)
Gold: Truth, enlightenment, splendor
White: purity, perfection, innocence, illumination, sacredness, simplicity, yang
Black: Void, death, time, night, cold, yin
Blue: Water, coolness, depth, space, heaven
Grey: Clouds, change, neutral (able to move into any direction), between dark and light
Green: Nature, abundance, spring (yellow + blue = green; i.e., warmth of emotions + coolness of wisdom = renewal, creativity

Crystal Insight, clarity

Cup Open, receptive, feminine, the heart

Dolphin Playfulness, intelligence, sensitivity, gentleness, joy

Eagle Inspiration, strength, authority, spiritual principal, a bridge between heaven and earth, masculine, solar, expansive

Eyes Open: Awareness

Closed: Inward looking, or asleepness

Fire Transformation, power, energy, strength, passion, purification, inspiration, masculine, solar

Flowers Full development of potentialities, expansion, open and sharing

Fruit Juiciness, fertility, essence

Hair Long flowing: Energy, freedom of thought (inspiration), life-force, virility
Shaved: Renouncing the physical
Disheveled: Confusion, unhappiness

Halo Light of truth, radiance, vital energy

Hand Empty: Open, receptive, feminine

Hara The center of vital energy in the body, just below the navel, life-force center

Jigsaw puzzle The game of life, the whole picture comprised of many small pieces

Knife/Sword Division, power, aggression, mental, cutting through (i.e., clarity)

Leaves Green: Fertility, regeneration
Autumn: Letting-go, maturity

Lightning Thunderbolt, revelation,

shock, divine power, enlightenment

Lion Fearlessness, power, individuality

Lizard Wisdom, secrecy, silence

Lotus Flower: The product of the union of opposites – light (sun) and dark (water), symbol of spirit and transformation Leaf: Perfection, spiritual unfoldment

Mantis Playfulness, non-serious inquiry

Monkey Transformation, trickster, curiosity

Moon Mystery, perpetual renewal (phases of), inner knowledge. Full moon: Enlightenment, feminine magnetism

Moon + Sun Heaven and earth, the sacred marriage, gold and silver

Night / Darkness Unknown, emptiness

No head No-mind – beyond thinking

Nudity Innocence, natural, unashamed

Octagon Number of regeneration, rebirth

Rainbow Bridge of heaven & earth, spiritual + manifest, full spectrum of possibilities

Rocks Challenges, barriers, inflexible

Rose Heart. Rose + thorns: Perfection/passion

Sheep Conditioning, status quo, 'the crowd'

Snake Rejuvenation, sexuality, cunning, totality, self-sufficiency, the end is the beginning

Spiral Fertility, the source of regeneration, a vortex, the creative force

Square The manifest, known, stable form

Sun Power, divinity, splendor, wisdom, illumination, masculine, source of life

Tiger Authority, wealth & accomplishment

Torch Life, truth, immortality, intelligence

Tortoise Self-contained, at home in water (emotions), on land (physical)

Tree Nourishing, rootedness, abundance, sheltering, stillness, strength, endurance

Triangle Threefold nature of the universe

  Upward pointing: Life, heat, male, King in court cards, spiritual

  Downward pointing: Lunar, feminine, receptive, Queen in court cards, cool

  Pointing left: Movement from the passive toward the active, Page in court cards

  Pointing right: Movement: the active

toward the inner, Knight in court cards

Veil Illusion, *maya,* darkness, ignorance

Venus Love, passion, creativity, femininity, imagination, sexuality

Wand /Staff Support, authority, journeying

Water Emotions, depth, intuition, flowing, the unmanifest, potential, purification, the womb and birth, life-giving

Wheel Time, fate, karma, change

Wings Freedom, flight into the unknown, the power to transcend the mundane

Wreath Of leaves, flowers, worn on head: Success, achievement over the material

Yin/Yang The complement of opposites. The black side – depth, darkness, unmanifest, soul, intuition, flexible, night, female The white side – active, day, male, manifest, expansive, rational. Together: a perfect balance of the two primary universal forces

Zodiac Cycle of transformation, interconnectedness of existence (heaven and earth), the world of phenomena

Osho's teachings defy categorization, covering everything from the individual quest for meaning to the most urgent social and political issues facing society today. His books are not written but are transcribed from audio and video recordings of extemporaneous talks given to international audiences over a period of thirty-five years. Osho has been described by the *Sunday Times* in London as one of the "1000 Makers of the Twentieth Century" and by American author Tom Robbins as "the most dangerous man since Jesus Christ."

About his own work Osho has said that he is helping to create the conditions for the birth of a new kind of human being. He has often characterized this new human being as "Zorba the Buddha" – capable both of enjoying the earthy pleasures of a Zorba the Greek and the silent serenity of a Gautam Buddha. Running like a thread through all aspects of Osho's work is a vision that encompasses both the timeless wisdom of the East and the highest potential of Western science and technology.

Osho is also known for his revolutionary contribution to the science of inner transformation, with an approach to meditation that acknowledges the accelerated pace of contemporary life. His unique "Osho Active Meditations" are designed to first release the accumulated stresses of body and mind, so it is easier to experience the thought-free and relaxed state of meditation.

See:
Autobiography of a Spiritually Incorrect Mystic, by Osho
320 pages; Publisher: St. Martin's Press / Griffin;

The Osho Meditation Resort is a great place for holidays and a place where people can have a direct personal experience of a new way of living with more alertness, relaxation, and fun. Located about one hundred miles southeast of Mumbai in Pune, India, the resort offers a variety of programs to thousands of people who visit each year from more than one hundred countries around the world.

Pune is a thriving modern city home to a number of universities and high-tech industries. The Meditation Resort spreads over forty acres in a tree-lined suburb known as Koregaon Park. The resort provides luxury guesthouse accommodation for visitors, with a plentiful variety of nearby hotels and private apartments available for stays of a few days up to several months.

All programs are based in the Osho vision of a qualitatively new kind of human being who is able both to participate creatively in everyday life and to relax into silence and meditation. Programs take place in modern, air-conditioned facilities and include introductions to meditation, especially trainings in Osho Active Meditations. Individual sessions, courses and workshops cover everything from creative arts to personal transformation, esoteric sciences, the "Zen" approach to sports and recreation.

Outdoor cafes and restaurants within the resort grounds serve both traditional Indian fare and a choice of international dishes, all made with organically grown vegetables from the resort's own farm. For more information and program descriptions see www.osho.com/resort.

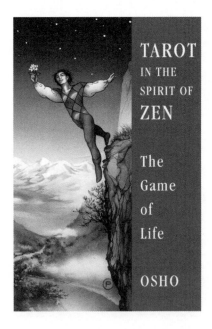

TAROT IN THE SPIRIT OF ZEN
The Game of Life
Osho

A unique and valuable resource for exploring the Zen approach to Tarot

A "must have" for owners of the phenomenally popular Osho Zen Tarot, this in-depth study of the meanings of the cards in the Osho Zen Tarot deck will also appeal to those who use the Rider, Crowley, and other, more traditional cards. The "here and now" approach of Zen offers the insight that the future evolves out of present events, ideas, and attitudes. Playful and accessible even to the novice, this remarkable handbook includes a table of correspondences for the Rider-Waite and Crowley decks, special sections on the meanings of the four major elements, or "suits" in the Tarot system.

US edition: St. Martin's Press, ISBN 0-312-31767-0
UK edition: Gill & Macmillan, ISBN 0 7171 3638 8

Deva Padma (Susan Morgan) is an American-born artist. Through meeting Osho she discovered, she says, that "Creativity is my meditation." For many years Padma lived as part of the community that surrounded Osho, contributing her artistic talent. The creation of the artwork for this Tarot was accomplished over four years with Osho's guidance and the insight and support of many members of the community. Special thanks go to Jivan Upasika who inspired the beginnings of this project in 1989, and who shared her extensive understanding of the Tarot.

1   *Dang Dang Doko Dang*, Ch. 2
2   *God is Dead: Now Zen is the Only Living Truth*, Ch. 1
3   *The Great Zen Master Ta Hui*, Ch. 23
4   *A Sudden Clash of Thunder*, Ch. 4
5   *The Zen Manifesto: Freedom from Oneself*, Ch. 9
6   *Take it Easy, Vol. 1*, Ch. 5
7   *Zen, Zest, Zip, Zap and Zing*, Ch. 3
8   *A Sudden Clash of Thunder*, Ch. 1
9   *Dang Dang Doko Dang*, Ch. 4
10 *The Discipline of Transcendence Vol. 1*, Ch. 2
11 *Take it Easy, Vol. 1*, Ch. 7
12 *Walking in Zen, Sitting in Zen*, Ch. 1
13 *Zen: The Diamond Thunderbolt*, Ch. 9
14 *Zen: The Solitary Bird, Cuckoo of the Forest*, Ch. 6
15 *Ancient Music in the Pines*, Ch. 1
16 *One Seed Makes the Whole Earth Green*, Ch. 4
17 *Isan: No Footprints in the Blue Sky*, Ch. 4
18 *Zen: The Diamond Thunderbolt*, Ch. 1
19 *Hyakujo: The Everest of Zen*, Ch. 7
20 *Dang Dang Doko Dang*, Ch. 7
21 *The Great Zen Master Ta Hui*, Ch. 12
22 *Joshu: The Lion's Roar*, Ch. 5
23 *Ah, This!*, Ch. 1
24 *Returning to the Source*, Ch. 8
25 *The Search: Talks on the Ten Bulls of Zen*, Ch. 2
26 *Zen: Turning In*, Ch. 10
27 *Nansen: The Point of Departure*, Ch. 8
28 *The Empty Boat*, Ch. 10
29 *A Sudden Clash of Thunder*, Ch. 5
30 *The Sun Rises in the Evening*, Ch. 9
31 *Christianity, the Deadliest Poison and Zen,
    the Antidote to all Poisons*, Ch. 6
32 *Dang Dang Doko Dang*, Ch. 5
33 *Bodhidharma, The Greatest Zen Master*, Ch. 15
34 *Take it Easy, Vol. 1*, Ch. 13
35 *The Sun Rises in the Evening*, Ch. 9
36 *Communism and Zen Fire, Zen Wind*, Ch. 2
37 *Christianity, the Deadliest Poison and Zen,
    the Antidote to all Poisons*, Ch. 5
38 *The Sun Rises in the Evening*, Ch. 7
39 *Dang Dang Doko Dang*, Ch. 7
40 *Live Zen*, Ch. 2

41   *Dang Dang Doko Dang*, Ch. 2
42   *Zen: The Miracle*, Ch. 2
43   *Take it Easy, Vol. 1*, Ch. 12
44   *Returning to the Source*, Ch. 4
45   *A Sudden Clash of Thunder*, Ch. 3
46   *Rinzai: Master of the Irrational*, Ch. 7
47   *Take it Easy, Vol. 1*, Ch. 13
48   *The Great Zen Master Ta Hui*, Ch. 20
49   *The Zen Manifesto: Freedom from Oneself*, Ch. 11
50   *The White Lotus*, Ch. 10
51   *I Celebrate Myself*, Ch. 4
52   *This Very Body The Buddha*, Ch. 9
53   *The Great Zen Master Ta Hui*, Ch. 10
54   *Take it Easy, Vol. 2*, Ch. 1
55   *Hsin Hsin Ming: The Book of Nothing*, Ch. 7
56   *The White Lotus*, Ch. 6
57   *A Sudden Clash of Thunder*, Ch. 8
58   *Dang Dang Doko Dang*, Ch. 3
59   *Take it Easy, Vol. 1*, Ch. 14
60   *Dang Dang Doko Dang*, Ch. 3
61   *Zen: The Path of Paradox, Vol. 1*, Ch. 5

62   *Dang Dang Doko Dang*, Ch. 8
63   *The Sun Rises in the Evening*, Ch. 4
64   *This Very Body The Buddha*, Ch. 6
65   *The White Lotus*, Ch. 10
66   *Take it Easy, Vol. 1*, Ch. 3
67   *Take it Easy, Vol. 2*, Ch. 12
68   *Live Zen*, Ch. 16
69   *Bodhidharma, the Greatest Zen Master*, Ch. 5
70   *The Great Zen Master Ta Hui*, Ch. 37
71   *God is Dead: Now Zen is the Only Living Truth*, Ch. 7
72   *Ancient Music in the Pines*, Ch. 2
73   *God is Dead: Now Zen is the Only Living Truth*, Ch. 3
74   *Dang Dang Doko Dang*, Ch. 4
75   *Zen: The Diamond Thunderbolt*, Ch. 10
76   *Dang Dang Doko Dang*, Ch. 3
77   *A Sudden Clash of Thunder*, Ch. 6
78   *I Celebrate Myself*, Ch. 4
79   *No Mind: The Flowers of Eternity*, Ch. 5

www.osho.com

A comprehensive Web site in several languages that includes an on-line tour of the Osho Meditation Resort and a calendar of its course offerings, a catalog of books and tapes, a list of Osho information centers worldwide, and selections from Osho's talks.

An online interactive version of the Osho Zen Tarot, plus information about software editions for *Palm* and *Pocket PC* devices can be found at www.osho.com/tarot.

Osho International
New York
Email: oshointernational@oshointernational.com
www.osho.com/oshointernational